CONSOLING THOUGHTS
of
ST. FRANCIS DE SALES

—FIRST BOOK—

*Consoling Thoughts on God,
Providence, the Saints, etc.*

CONSOLING THOUGHTS
of
ST. FRANCIS DE SALES

—FIRST BOOK—

Consoling Thoughts on God,
Providence, the Saints, etc.

Gathered from His Writings,
And Arranged in Order, by the
REV. PÈRE HUGUET

TRANSLATED FROM THE FRENCH

27TH EDITION

"You cannot read anything more useful than the works of
St. Francis de Sales, in which everything is pleasing
and consoling."—Fenelon

TAN Books
An Imprint of Saint Benedict Press, LLC
Charlotte, North Carolina

Published by Fr. Pustet & Co., New York & Cincinnati, Printer to the Holy See and the S. Congregation of Rites, in 1912, under the title *The Consoling Thoughts of St. Francis de Sales*. A French edition of this work, apparently an earlier edition, was published in Paris in 1857 as *Pensees consolantes de Saint Francois de Sales*. . . . The compiler's surname is sometimes spelled Hoguet; his first name was given as Paul in the French edition. Retypeset in 2013 by TAN Books.

Cover design by Caroline Kiser.

Cover image: *The Creation of the World* (oil on canvas), Le Sueur, Eustache (1617–55) / Musee des Beaux-Arts, Tourcoing, France / Giraudon / The Bridgeman Art Library

ISBN: 978-0-89555-211-2

Printed and bound in the United States of America.

TAN Books
An Imprint of Saint Benedict Press, LLC
Charlotte, North Carolina
2013

ST. FRANCIS DE SALES' LOVING HEART

"Through a great part of my soul I am poor and weak, but I have a boundless and almost immutable affection for those who favor me with their friendship. Whoever challenges me in the contest of friendship must be very determined, for I spare no effort. There is no person in the world who has a heart more tender and affectionate towards his friends than I, or one who feels a separation more acutely."
—St. Francis de Sales.

"It has pleased God to make my heart thus. I wish to love this dear neighbor ever so much—ever so much I wish to love him! Oh! When shall we be all melted away in meekness and charity towards our neighbor! I have given him my whole person, my means, my affections, that they may serve him in all his wants."—St. Francis de Sales.

CONTENTS

PUBLISHER'S PREFACE

—————————

ST. FRANCIS de Sales was a man of great passion.
Reading his thought is to know his heart. Has Holy
Mother Church ever reared a child so willing and able to
express his longing for perfect union with God? Has a man
so learned ever presented Truth and Beauty so simply?

Words cannot fully express the Publisher's apprecia-
tion for this Gentle Saint, the Bishop of Geneva and Doctor of the Church. Saint Francis was a lawyer, a theologian,
and a missionary. As a young priest, he volunteered to re-
evangelize the Calvinist of Chablais, France. He preached
not only with conviction, but also with unparalleled gentleness and grace. He worked tirelessly, even under the cover
of night, slipping his apologetic writings beneath the doors
of anti-Catholics. The Lord rewarded him with one of the
most remarkable and well-documented events in Catholic
history when nearly the entire population of 72,000 Cal-
vinists returned to the Faith.

This volume, *Consoling Thoughts*, is representative
of why St. Francis was so well-received in Chablais, and

indeed, throughout history. Perhaps more than any other saint, St. Francis preached truth with love. His teachings, his works, and his very presence were consoling to those 72,000 lost souls of Chablais and to millions of more over the centuries. Now, then, it is our hope that they will offer consolation to a new generation of Catholics.

It is for this reason that TAN Books is proud to bring this compilation of St. Francis' writings back to print. Initially published in a single volume, we now present this work in a four volume series, carefully arranged by topic to give solace in times of darkness, or, simply in times of deep meditation.

It is the Publisher's sincere hope that *Consoling Thoughts* finds a permanent home in your library and among our long list of Saint Francis de Sales classics, including *Introduction to the Devout Life*, *Treatise on the Love of God*, *Catholic Controversies*, and *Sermons of St. Francis de Sales* (in four volumes).

Saint Francis de Sales, Doctor of the Church, *Pray For Us.*

Robert M. Gallagher, Publisher
November 19, 2012

PREFACE TO THE SIXTH FRENCH EDITION

By Père Huguet

SIX editions of this little work, published in a short time, tell better than any words of ours the popularity which St. Francis de Sales enjoys amongst us. Many sick and wounded souls have found in these sweet and affecting pages a heavenly consolation.

Encouraged by this success, the honor of which belongs to God and His blessed servant, we have again with pen in hand run through the works of the Bishop of Geneva, to glean carefully whatever had escaped us on our former tour. Nor has our labor been in vain; we have gathered new flowers, whose beauty and perfume yield in no respect to the first.[1] To introduce them in this edition, we have been obliged to lop off a good many of the old chapters which were so well suited to the object of the book. We have acted thus with the less regret as we have published the omitted

---

1   The author has scarcely taken anything from the *Introduction to a Devout Life,* this admirable book being in the hands of everyone.

portions, complete, in two other volumes: the *Consoling Piety of St. Francis de Sales,* and the *Month of Immaculate Mary, by St. Francis de Sales.* These two works form a complete course of consolation for all the trials of life.

We may be permitted to give a short extract from a late number of the *Catholic Bibliography,* which contained an article on *Consoling Thoughts.* The idea of publishing the article was most remote from our mind, on account of the many marks of very great kindness towards us which it bears; but remembering that the merit of this work belongs entirely to St. Francis de Sales, we have felt impelled to give at least an extract, as a new and encouraging proof of the opportuneness of our little book.

"The very title of the book," it says "pleases, and should secure a large number of readers. How many souls are there today who stand in need of being encouraged and consoled? Want of confidence is the great obstacle in the work of the Christian apostleship. Discouragement is the evil of our period, because in general the Christian life, or SANCTITY, appears like a sharp mountain, which only few persons can ascend; in despair of arriving at its summit the majority of men remain below on the plains. The mere word 'sanctity' frightens. The *Lives of the Saints,* which ought to encourage, often discourage, by their list of heroic virtues; we gladly conclude that such a state of perfection is suited only to a very small number, and we remain out of the ways of sanctity for fear of not being able to walk in them.

"Blessed then be the pious author who has received the happy inspiration of assembling together the *Consoling Thoughts of St. Francis de Sales,* the sweetest and most amiable of the saints, and one of the greatest masters of the spiritual life!

"It is especially by his admirable union of firmness and mildness that St. Francis de Sales shines in the first rank of ascetic writers. Who else ever painted virtue under lovelier colors, or made it easier or more practicable? Whoever knew better how to enlighten and bring back souls that had withdrawn from God, or that wearied themselves in His service by an unreasonable fear?

"Happy then and useful inspiration [it was], to gather from his works the thoughts most fitted to enlighten pious and timorous souls, to console them, and to dilate their hearts dried up by fear! Father Huguet has given us, in this little work, the quintessence of everything that our amiable saint wrote most sweet and consoling, especially in his letters, in which that heart so good and tender, which God had formed to comfort the afflicted, is entirely revealed. The book is of the greatest assistance to the simple faithful, and to directors and confessors charged with comforting discouraged and troubled souls.

"A word now as to the method adopted. The author read, he tells us, with pen in hand, the works of the holy Bishop of Geneva; and, after noting the different passages which referred to the same subject, he arranged them in such order as to form a single chapter. A page is thus sometimes collected from seven or eight places in the saint's writings. Yet such is the connection of ideas that we scarcely perceive the labor, and everything seems to flow as from one fountainhead. As to the graceful, artless style of St. Francis de Sales, the author has lightly retouched it in some places, changing a few antiquated expressions that would be little intelligible nowadays. Without altering anything in substance, he has considered it a duty to suppress certain details and comparisons, whose want of simplicity, a common fault at present, might cloy the work. Everywhere we have the good shepherd, who, after the example of his Divine Master, instructs, cheers, and consoles, by the help of parables and similitudes, in the great art of using which perhaps he never had an equal.

"To add more clearness and authority to the book, the author has, from time to time, placed at the foot of the page some notes taken from the most esteemed writings of our greatest masters of the spiritual life, particularly Bossuet and Fenelon. These notes, happily selected, give a new value to the work. Should we now recommend it to all those whose souls have need to be encouraged and consoled—in a word, all the faithful?"

INTRODUCTION

By Père Huguet

"The writings of St. Francis de Sales are the fruit
of grace and experience."—Fenelon

THE great evil of our period is discouragement. Tempers and characters have become weak and degenerate. Everyone agrees in saying that the most common obstacle, and the one most difficult to be overcome, which all those meet who labor for the conversion of sinners and the sanctification of pious souls, is want of confidence. The great evil that Jansenism wrought in the midst of us has not yet entirely disappeared: many still believe that perfection consists only in fearing the Lord and in trembling before Him, who, in His mercy, permits us to call Him *Our Father,* and to name Him *the good God.*

The generality of authors have placed in the *Lives of the Saints* an account of their heroic virtues only, without a single word of the defects and miseries which God left in them, in order to preserve them in humility and to make them more indulgent towards their brethren; yet the history of their weaknesses would, according to the judicious remark of St. Francis de Sales, have done the greatest good to a large number of souls, who imagine that sanctity can, and should, be exempt, even in this world, from all alloy and all imperfection. It is to remedy, as far as lies in our power, these inconveniences, that we have gathered together, under appropriate headings, from the writings of the sweetest and most amiable of all the saints, those passages which are best calculated to enlighten pious souls, and to expand their hearts withered with fear.

The writings of St. Francis de Sales are admirably suited to times of trial and sadness. The soul enjoys in them an atmosphere of mild salubrity that strengthens and renews it. The doctrine there is holy and profound, under a most amiable exterior; the style adds, by its simple naïveté, to the charm of a clear and ingenuous fancy; we are instructed while we imagine ourselves distracted, and admire while we smile.

We hesitate not to say that no saint has ever contributed so much as St. Francis de Sales, by his immortal writings, to make piety loved and practiced in all classes of society.

"Under his pen," says the best of his biographers, "devotion is noble, true and rational; courtesy of manners, a spirit of sociality, all the charms of a well-ordered piety, form its cortege, if we may use the expression, and yet it is not disguised in order to appear the more agreeable. Everywhere the author's sweetness appears without weakness, and his firmness without bitterness. He teaches us to respect decorum, which he calls the gracefulness of virtue, to rise above nature without destroying it, to fly little by little towards Heaven like doves when we cannot soar thither like eagles, that is to say, to sanctify ourselves by ordinary means. There the mind contemplates truth, unveiled in majestic splendor, bedecked with maxims equally elegant and profound, clad in a style noble, flowing and natural, relieved by the justness of the expressions, sometimes fine and delicate, sometimes vivid and impressive, always graceful and varied: this is simplicity, with all the merit of beauty, for every idea is rendered by the proper word, and every word embellishes the thought. There, above all, the heart tastes an inexpressible pleasure; because the sweetness of the sentiment always seasons the precept, while the delicacy of the precaution that accompanies it secures its acceptance, and the artless candor and goodness of the author, who paints himself without intending it, make him beloved; at the same time the soul, embalmed in what it reads, deliciously participates in the sweetest and purest perfume of true piety."[1]

The style of St. Francis de Sales is a picture of his heart as much as of his mind: we feel that he loves and deserves to be loved, but that he wishes above all things that we should love God.

A special characteristic of St. Francis de Sales is that the frequent use he makes of figures and the comparisons which he endlessly multiplies, never weary. This style would be clumsy in another author; with our saint it is a

---

1   *Life of St. Francis de Sales,* by M. the Curé of Saint Sulpice. This beautiful work has met with a success which surprises no one except its author, whose modesty and evangelical simplicity can alone equal his learning and his zeal for the conversion of souls.

new pleasure, which draws away the reader and attracts him every moment, as a gentle magnet, and this with so much the more ease as the reader does not perceive it. One is led along unresistingly, yielding with pleasure to the charms of this enchanting style. An effect, so rare and wonderful, is owing not only to our saint's judicious choice of figures and comparisons, but also to his amiable character, to the sprightliness of his sentiments, and to the transports of his love for God, which burst forth even in the midst of the most abstract truths. He cannot contain the fire that consumes him; he allows it to escape by every sense. Moreover, he so well unites simplicity of diction with beauty of metaphor, that, in perusing his works, we feel the ornaments to flow from his pen without an effort on his part to seek them. A tender and compassionate soul, he is full of charity towards his friends. Let us hear him speak: "Through a great part of my soul I am poor and weak, but I have a boundless and almost immutable affection for those who favor me with their friendship. Whoever challenges me in the contest of friendship must be very determined, for I spare no effort. There is no person in the world who has a heart more tender and affectionate towards his friends than I, or one who feels a separation more acutely."

We have so often heard the following affecting words repeated, that they seem to have fallen from the mouth of the sweet Saviour Himself: "It has pleased God to make my heart thus. I wish to love this dear neighbor ever so much—ever so much I wish to love him! Oh, when shall we be all melted away in meekness and charity towards our neighbor! I have given him my whole person, my means, my affections, that they may serve him in all his wants."

This benignity, this gentleness, which breathed through the whole conduct of our saint, made St. Vincent de Paul exclaim with touching simplicity: "O my God! How good must Thou be, since the Bishop of Geneva is so good!"

It is in his works that he deposited the richest treasures of this sweet sensibility and of this playful imagination, which enabled him to lend to the driest subjects and the severest precepts of the evangelic law a charm that makes them loved even by the profane.

The French Academy proposed the writings of St. Francis de Sales as a model to all, even at a time when it extolled the faults of Corneille.

To make himself all to all, St. Francis de Sales descends to the level of the simple faithful, and there he loves to rest. Sometimes he places himself with his *Philothea* in the midst of the stormy sea of the world, and there casts out the anchor of faith; again, he takes his stand on the high road to show to the multitude, who pass indifferent and distracted along, the narrow way that leads to Heaven. We might say that he smoothes its roughness, so carefully does he conceal it under flowers. These are not deceitful flowers, by which virtue is disfigured in the endeavor to render it more attractive; they are those flowers of the soul which perfume without corrupting it, secret joys, interior consolations, ineffable delights, the anticipated inheritance of God's elect upon earth. The picture which he draws of devotion can only be compared to that of charity by St. Paul. "In his writings," says Père de Tournemine, "we have the morality of the Sacred Scriptures and the Holy Fathers reduced to true principles and practical rules."

The doctrine of St. Francis de Sales is like a beautiful river which takes its rise in pure and elevated regions, and which, descending to the lowlands, spreads wide its banks, in order to reflect a broader expanse of Heaven; it is decked with the flowers of the prairie which it gathers on its course, and carries to the sea a tribute only of limpid and perfumed waters.

According to St. Francis de Sales, we must not be too punctilious in the practice of virtues, but approach them honestly, with liberty, in a *grosso modo* way. "Walk simply in the way of the Lord," he says, "and do not torment your mind. We must hate our defects, but with a tranquil and quiet hatred—not with a spiteful and troubled hatred— and, if necessary, have patience to witness them and to turn them to account by a holy self-abasement. For want of this, my daughter, your imperfections, which you view so closely, trouble you much, and by this means are retained, there being nothing that better preserves our defects than fretfulness and anxiety to remove them." (*Sermon for the Feast of St. Magdalen*).

He applies to himself what he counsels to others: "I know what sort of a being I am; yet even though I feel myself miserable, I am not troubled at it; nay, I am sometimes joyful at it, considering that I am a truly fit object for the mercy of God, to which I continually recommend you."

This devotion, at least in appearance so easy, naturally pleases persons of the world, who, like the Count

Bussy-Rabutin, say: "I merely wish to get into Heaven, and no higher." This nobleman, writing in another place, says: "Save us with our good Francis de Sales; he conducted people to Heaven by beautiful ways." Yet these beautiful ways were no other than the narrow way of which the Gospel speaks; only our amiable saint knew how to smooth its entrance and to hide its thorns under flowers.

St. Francis particularly excelled in comforting the afflicted and the sick; a few words falling from his heart sufficed to calm and enlighten them; his words entered into their soul as an oil of great sweetness, which moderated the heat of their malady. Let us hear him console a pious person to whom sickness was an insupportable burden: "Be not annoyed to remain in bed without meditation, for to endure the scourges of Our Lord is no less a good than to meditate. No, indeed; but it is much better to be on the cross with Jesus Christ, than merely to contemplate Him in prayer." To another, who was troubled at the sight of her miseries, he said: "When we happen to fall, let us cast down our heart before God, to say to Him, in a spirit of confidence and humility, 'Mercy, Lord! For I am weak.' Let us arise in peace, unite again the thread of our affections, and continue our work."

St. Francis de Sales was so much the better qualified to tranquilize and encourage souls inclined to diffidence and depression, as he had himself been obliged to pass through the severest trials, and arrived at the possession of peace of heart only by a total abandonment to God. "Since at every season of life, early or late, in youth or in old age, I can expect my salvation from the pure goodness and mercy of God alone, it is much better to cast myself from this moment into the arms of His clemency than to wait till another time. The greater part of the journey is over; let the Lord do with me according to His will; my fate is in His hands; let Him dispose of me according to His good pleasure."

The pious M. Olier, that great master of the spiritual life, very much esteemed St. Francis de Sales. "God," he says, "wishing to raise him up as a torch in the midst of His Church to enlighten an immense number, replenished him with the most marvelous gifts of understanding, knowledge, and wisdom, proportioned to His designs. As for his knowledge, it was evidently more than human, and the effect of the Divine Spirit."

If you wish to know Francis de Sales thoroughly, to be initiated into the most secret mysteries of that vast understanding and that perfect heart, read and re-read his *Letters,* in which every subject, from the most humble to the most sublime, from a simple how-do-you-do to a description of ecstasies and eternal beatitudes, is treated of in the style that best suits it. Read, above all, the *Letters to Madame de Chantal,* and those which treat of the *direction of souls.* Considering these admirable letters, Bossuet says: "Francis de Sales is truly sublime; there is no one among moderns with such sweetness, who has a hand so steady and experienced as his, to elevate souls to perfection and to detach them from themselves." The letter written after the death of his mother is of a primitive simplicity, and a sublime model of Christian resignation; we imagine that we hear St. Augustine weeping over St. Monica, and the tears it makes us shed have nothing of bitterness, so sweet is the death of the just when thus related.

The learned and pious Archbishop of Cambray continually recommended the perusal of our saint's writings. "You cannot read anything more useful," says Fenelon, "than the books of St. Francis de Sales; everything there is consoling and pleasing, though he does not say a word but to help us to die. His artless style displays an amiable simplicity, which is above all, the flourishes of the profane writer. You see a man who, with great penetration and a perfect clearness of mind to judge of the reality of things, and to know the human heart, desires only to speak as a good-natured friend, to console, to solace, to enlighten, to perfect his neighbor. No person was better acquainted than he with the highest perfection; but he repeated himself for the little, and never disdained anything, however small. He made himself all to all, not to please all, but to gain all, and to gain them to Jesus Christ, not to himself."

To this judgment of the pious Bishop of Cambray we shall add that of the learned Bourdaloue: "The doctrine of St. Francis de Sales is a food, not of earth, but of Heaven, which, from the same substance, nourishes, like the manna, all kinds of persons; and I am able to say, without offending against the respect which I owe to all other writers, that after the Holy Scriptures there are no works that have better maintained piety among the faithful than those of this holy bishop."

The illustrious Monsignore of Paris shared the same sentiments. "All that can contribute," he says, "to make the most amiable of saints better known to the world must be useful to the cause of our holy religion."

Thus, the three men who were the glory of the clergy of France in the age of Louis XIV were unanimous in esteeming and praising the works of this great master of the spiritual life.

Protestants themselves are obliged to render justice to the exceptional merit of the works of St. Francis de Sales. One of their best authors[2] thus appreciates the writings of the blessed Bishop of Geneva: "From its first appearance, the *Introduction to a Devout Life* had a universal success in France, and editions succeeded one another rapidly. This was an event of great consequence in regard to such a book, and Catholicism could most justly rejoice at it. The learned controversies of Bellarmine had been of far less advantage: they had indeed fitted for theological discussion a clergy who found themselves face to face with superior forces; but from the first blow, the *Introduction* could make conquests to a religion whose practices were presented under forms so amiable, and even so delightful. . . . Among Calvinistic gentlemen solicited to abjure their faith, the little book served as an occasion for more than one renunciation. In this respect, the *Introduction to a Devout Life* was, in the beginning of the century, what the *Exposition of the Catholic Faith* was in the middle, and had effects quite similar. Of all that St. Francis de Sales has written, his *Letters* are the most widely spread: Protestants read them after a selection, for all would not suit their taste; but in each class,

---

2 *History of French Literature*, by M. Sayous.

the amiable and glowing piety, the grace—what shall I say? The wit, the familiar gossip, with which the Bishop allows his pen to twirl along, have a singular charm; and never does the afflicted or dejected heart disdain the consolation and encouragement which it finds in perusing them."

It is in his correspondence that we must study the great, the holy Bishop of Geneva; there we shall find humility unparalleled, a joyous cordiality, peace unutterable, the sole desire of accomplishing the will of God.

There we shall find that elegance, ever new, in thought and in expression; that richness of beautiful images and of fine comparisons borrowed from things most familiar: the rose, the pigeon, the halcyon, the bee, the odorous plants of Arabia; that dovelike simplicity, that childlike candor which does not, however, exclude, on due occasions, a manly strength and energy; that chaste tenderness which could only come from Heaven; that gentle meekness which holds the key of every heart.

We shall be the less surprised at the eulogies given to the writings of St. Francis de Sales by the most experienced doctors and the most eminent personages, when we consider with what maturity and wisdom they were composed. Those beautiful pages, which seem to flow as from a well, so free and natural are the doctrine and the style, are the fruit of the most serious study and the most assiduous meditation, joined with a great knowledge of the human heart, which he had acquired in the direction of souls.[3]

His beautiful *Treatise on the Love of God* is the result

---

3   *Spirit of St. Francis de Sales.*

of twenty-four years' preaching, according to the statement of the author himself, and the fruit of such profound study, that there are fourteen lines in it, which, as he told Mgr. Camus, Bishop of Belley, had cost him the reading of more than twelve hundred pages in folio.[4] After this, we should not be surprised at the unexampled success which has crowned the writings of St. Francis de Sales. The *Treatise on the Love of God* is a most beautiful book, and one that has had a great circulation. All the agitations, all the inconsistencies of the human heart are painted in it with inimitable art. We behold there the exercises of love, contemplation, the repose of the soul in God, its languors, its transports, its dereliction, its dying sadness, its return to courage, the abandonment of the docile spirit to the secret ways of Providence. When the *Introduction to a Devout Life* appeared in the world, it created an extraordinary sensation; everyone wished to procure it, to read it, and, having read it, to read it again. Very soon it was translated into nearly all the languages of Europe, and editions succeeded one another so rapidly that in 1656 it had reached the fortieth. Henry IV, on reading it, declared that the work far surpassed his expectations; Mary of Medici, his wife, sent it bound in diamonds and precious stones to James, King of England; and this monarch, one of the most learned who ever occupied a throne, conceived such an esteem for it, that, notwithstanding his schismatical and spiteful prejudices against Catholic writers, he carried it always about

---

4   It is related that the publisher, in gratitude for the considerable gain he had derived from the sale of the *Introduction to a Devout Life,* made a journey to Annecy expressly to offer as a gift to the author a sum of four hundred crowns of gold. (*Memoirs of the Academic Society of Savoy,* Vol. II).

with him and often read it. Many times he was heard to say: "Oh, how I should wish to know the author! He is certainly a great man, and among all our bishops there is not one capable of writing in this manner, which breathes of Heaven and the angels." The general of the Feuillants, speaking of this work, calls it the most perfect book that mortal hand ever composed, a book that one would always wish to read again after having read it many times, and he adds this beautiful eulogium, that in reading it he who would not be a Christian should become better, and he who would be better should become perfect.[5]

The Church, directed by the Holy Spirit, exhorts all her children to be guided by the counsels of St. Francis de Sales. *Admonished by his directions,* she says in his Office. She assures us that his works have diffused a bright light amongst the faithful, to whom they point out a way as sure as it is easy, to arrive at perfection.

We could, if our design permitted it, multiply evidence in favor of the works of St. Francis de Sales. We shall terminate this introduction by some extracts from a letter of Pope Alexander VII, one of the greatest of his panegyrists: "I conjure you anew to make the works of M. de Sales your delight and your dearest study. I have read them I cannot tell how many times, and I would not dispense myself from reading them again; they never lose the charm of novelty; they always seem to me to say something more than they had said before. If you trust me, these writings should be the mirror of your life, and the rule by which to form your

---

5 *Life of St. Francis de Sales,* by M. the Abbé Hamon.

every action and your every thought. As for me, I confess to you that from often reading them I have become like a repository of his most beautiful sentiments and the principal points of his doctrine, that I ruminate over them at my leisure, that I taste them, and that I make them, so to speak, pass into my very blood and substance. Such is my opinion of this great saint, exhorting you with all my heart to follow him."

If in gathering these lovely flowers and binding them into bunches, we have lessened their beauty or their perfume, we trust that still they will at least a little serve those severely tried souls for whom we intend them; we shall consider it an ample recompense for all our trouble, if, even in a single heart, they increase confidence in God, and the desire to love and serve Him generously.

"Most holy Mother of God, the most lovable, the most loving, and the most loved, of creatures! Prostrate at thy feet, I dedicate and consecrate to thee this little work of love, in honor of the immense greatness of thy love. O Jesus! To whom could I more fitly offer these words of Thy love than to the most amiable heart of the well-beloved of Thy soul?"[6]

---

6   Dedication of the *Treatise on the Love of God,* by St. Francis de Sales.

—First Book—

*Consoling Thoughts on God,
Providence, the Saints, etc.*

CHAPTER ONE

THE INCLINATION GOD
HAS TO DO US GOOD

AS SOON as man thinks attentively on the Divinity, he perceives a certain sweet emotion of heart which testifies that God is the God of the human heart; and never does our understanding experience more pleasure than in this thought of the Divinity, the least knowledge of which, as the prince of the philosophers says, is more precious than the greatest of all things else: as the least ray of the sun is brighter than the brightest of the moon or of the stars, yea, is more luminous than the moon and stars together. And if any accident surprises our heart, immediately it has recourse to the Divinity, acknowledging that when the world looks dark, It alone is good, and when danger threatens, It alone can save and preserve.

This pleasure, this confidence, which the human heart naturally takes in God, can only proceed from the conformity that exists between the Divine Goodness and the soul. There is a great, but secret, resemblance between them—a resemblance that cannot be denied, yet cannot be understood. We are created to the image of God, we have a close connection with His Divine Majesty.

Besides this conformity, there is a constant intercourse between God and man for their reciprocal perfection. Not that God can receive any perfection from man, but because, as man can be perfected only by the Divine Goodness, so the Divine Goodness can nowhere outside of itself be so well displayed as in regard to our humanity. The one has great need and capacity to receive, the other great abundance and inclination to bestow. Nothing is more suited to indigence than affluence; and the kinder affluence is, the stronger its inclination to give. The more needy indigence is, the more eager it is to be satiated. The meeting, then, of affluence and indigence is sweet and happy; and we could scarcely say which should enjoy the more contentment, abundance to be communicated, or deficiency to be filled, had not Our Lord told us that it is a more blessed thing to give than to receive. But where there is more of happiness, there is more of satisfaction; the Divine Goodness, then, has greater pleasure in giving its graces, than we have in receiving them.

Mothers have sometimes their paps so full that they cannot refrain from presenting them to an infant; and while one takes the breast with avidity, the other yields it yet more willingly; the infant drinking, pressed by its necessity, and the mother supplying drink, pressed by her fecundity.[1]

---

1   "To make you better understand by sound doctrine how immense is the mercy of Our Lord, I beg you to consider a truth which I have taken from Tertullian. This

Thus our deficiency has need of the divine abundance through the misery of its dearth, but the divine affluence has no need of our indigence, unless through the perfection of its goodness: a goodness which, nevertheless, does not become better by being communicated, for it acquires nothing by expending itself; but our indigence would remain failing, if the abundance of the Divine Goodness did not succor it.

Has not our soul then—considering that nothing can perfectly content it, that its capacity cannot be filled by anything in this world, that its understanding has an infinite longing after more extensive knowledge, and its will an insatiable desire to find and love what is good—has it not reason to exclaim: Ah! I am not made for this world! There is some sovereign good on which I depend, some infinite Creator who has placed within me this boundless desire of knowing and this hunger which cannot be satisfied. It is therefore necessary that I should tend forward and stretch out towards Him in order to be united to His goodness, to which I belong. Such is the conformity that we have with God.

---

great man teaches us that God began His works by an outpouring of His goodness on all His creatures, and that His first inclination is to do us good. And indeed, it appears to me that the reason is quite evident; for to know well what the first inclination is, we must select that which should be the most natural, inasmuch as nature is the root of all. But is there anything more natural in our God, than to enrich us with the profusion of His graces?

"As a fountain sends out its waters naturally, as the sun sends forth its rays naturally, so God does good naturally: being good and abounding in riches by His natural condition, He should also be by nature liberal and beneficent. When He punishes you, O wicked man! The reason is not in Himself; He does not wish that any person should perish; it is your malice, your ingratitude, that draws down His indignation upon your head."—*Bossuet.*

CHAPTER TWO

THE ETERNAL LOVE OF GOD FOR US

CONSIDER the eternal love which God has borne towards you; for already, long before Jesus Christ had suffered for you on the cross as man, His Divine Majesty destined you to life and loved you infinitely. But when did He begin to love you? When He began to be God. And when did He begin to be God? Never; He has always been, without beginning and without end; and thus He has always loved you, and it is from all eternity that His love prepared for you the graces and favors which He has given you. He says by the prophet: "I have loved thee," (speaking to you as to everyone else) "with an everlasting love, and I have mercifully drawn thee to Me." Among other things, He has thought of making you take good resolutions to love and serve Him.[1]

---

1 "The Divine Goodness and justice are like two arms to God; but goodness is the right arm, which begins and accomplishes almost everything, and which He wishes

Oh, how amiable is this great God who, of His infinite goodness, has given His Son as a redemption for the whole world! Yes, alas! For all in general, but still in particular for me, *who am the chief of sinners*. Ah! *He loved me;* I say, He loved me, me, that is myself, such as I am, *and delivered Himself* to His Passion *for me*.

We must consider the divine benefits in their first and eternal origin. O God![2] My Theotime, how can we have worthy or sufficient love for the infinite goodness of our Creator, who from all eternity designed to create us, to preserve, govern, redeem, save, and glorify, all in general, and each one of us in particular? Who was I when I was not—I, I say, who, being now something, am nothing but a mere contemptible worm of the earth? And yet God, from the abyss of His eternity, *thought thoughts* of benediction on me. Thus He meditated and appointed the hour of my birth, of my Baptism, of all the inspirations which He would give me, and in a word of all the benefits which He would bestow upon and offer me.[3] Alas! Is there any sweetness like this sweetness?

---

to appear in all His works. If men allowed it to guide them, it would load them with benefits in keeping with its munificence. There is a sort of division between goodness and justice: all beginnings belong to goodness; thus all things in their first institution are very good. Justice extends only to what is added, which is sin. But there is this difference, that justice never takes anything from the rights of goodness. On the contrary, goodness sometimes anticipates those of justice; for, by pardon, it is exercised upon sins, which are the proper matter for justice."—*Bossuet.*

2   "O God!"—a devout expression that is characteristic of St. Francis de Sales, who lived and spoke in the presence of God.—*Publisher, 2013.*

3   "Goodness is united in God to omnipotence; this is a truth often repeated in the prayers of the holy liturgy: 'Lord! Thou art good and all-powerful!' So long as the soul is not well convinced of this union of goodness and power in God, it has only half-strength, half-love, an imperfect idea of the divine succor, from which we should expect all things. Yet a faith that fears nothing is necessary for souls who desire courageously to imitate Jesus Christ; let them learn, therefore, how to hope for everything."—*Père de Ravignan.*

In its love and mercy the Divine Goodness prepared all means, general and particular, for our salvation. Yes, indeed, as a mother prepares the cradle, the linens, the swathing bands, and even a nourishment, for the infant to which she is about to give birth, so Our Lord, in the desire of bringing us forth to salvation and of making us His children, prepared on the tree of the cross all that was requisite for us: our spiritual cradle, our linens, our swathing bands, our nourishment, and all else that was necessary for us. These are the means, the attractions, the graces, by which He conducts our souls and draws them to His perfection.

We must consider the divine benefits in their second meritorious source; for do you not know, Theotime, that the high priest of the Law carried on his shoulders and breast the names of the children of Israel, that is to say, precious stones on which the names of the chiefs of Israel were engraved? Behold Jesus, our great *Bishop,* and look upon Him from the moment of His conception; consider that He carries us on His shoulders, accepting the charge of redeeming us by His death, *even the death of the cross.* O Theotime, Theotime! This soul of the Saviour knew us all by our name and our surname; but, above all, on the day of His Passion, when He offered His tears, His prayers, His blood, and His life for us all, He darted forth in particular for you these thoughts of love: "Alas! O my Eternal Father, I take upon me and charge myself with all the sins of poor Theotime, to suffer torments and death, that he may be acquitted of them, and that he may not perish, but may live. May I die, provided he lives! May I be crucified, provided he be glorified!" O sovereign love

Heart of Jesus, what heart can ever praise Thee
...iently?

Thus, within His breast, maternal breast, the divine
Heart foresaw, arranged, merited, and impetrated all the
blessings we possess, not only in general for all, but in particular for each one; and His paps of sweetness prepared
for us the milk of His motions, His inspirations, and His
sweetnesses, by which He draws, conducts, and nourishes
our souls to eternal life. Benefits will not affect us, if we
do not regard the eternal Will that destined them, and the
Heart of the Saviour that merited them for us by so many
pains, especially during His Passion and death.

The Divine Love, seated on the Heart of the Saviour, as on a royal throne, beholds through the window
of His pierced side all the hearts of the children of men;
for Our Lord, being the King of Hearts, keeps His eyes
always fixed on hearts. But as those who look through lat-
tices see and are not seen, so the divine love of this Heart,
or rather the Heart of this divine love, always sees ours
clearly, but we do not see it, we only get a glimpse of it. For,
O God! If we were to see it as it is, we should die of love
for it.

Adore its sovereign goodness, which from all eternity
named you by your name, and designed to save you, destin-
ing for you amid a variety of things the present day, that on
it you might perform works of piety and salvation, according to what has been said by the prophet: "I have loved thee
with an everlasting love; therefore have I drawn thee, taking
pity on thee."

On account of this thought, you ought to unite your

will with that of our most benign and merciful heavenly Father, in these or suchlike words, cordially uttered: O most sweet will of my God, be ever done! O eternal designs of the will of my God, I adore you, and consecrate and dedicate to you my will, to will eternally what You have eternally willed! Oh, may I then do this day, and always, and in all things, Thy divine will, my sweet Creator! Yes, heavenly Father! For such has been Thy pleasure from all eternity. Amen. O most agreeable goodness, may it be as Thou hast willed! O eternal will, live and reign in my will forever.

O God! What resolutions are like those on which God has thought and meditated from all eternity! How dear and precious they should be to us! How much we ought to suffer rather than lose any of them! No, indeed, we ought not to lose any of them, though the whole world should perish; for all the world together is not worth one soul, and our soul is worth nothing without its resolutions.

O dear resolutions, you are the beautiful tree of life which God has planted with His hand in the midst of my heart, and which my Saviour wishes to water with His blood to make it fructify; I prefer a thousand deaths rather than permit anyone to root you up. No, neither vanity, nor delights, nor tribulations shall ever make me change my intentions.

Ah, Lord! Thou hast planted this beautiful tree, after having kept it eternally in Thy paternal bosom, to transfer it at length into my garden. How many souls there are that have not been so favored! And how can I humble myself sufficiently under the hand of Thy mercy?

O beautiful and holy resolutions, if I preserve you, you will preserve me; if you live in my soul, my soul will live in you. Live then forever in me, as you have been eternally in the mercy of God, and may I be ever faithful to you!

CHAPTER THREE

CONFIDENCE IN GOD FOUNDED
ON THE CONSIDERATION OF
OUR OWN MISERY

NOT only can the soul that knows its misery have a great confidence in God, but it cannot have a true confidence unless it has a knowledge of its misery; for this knowledge and confession of our misery introduce us to God. Thus all the great saints, Job, David, and the rest, began their prayers by the acknowledgment of their misery and unworthiness; so that it is a most excellent thing to own oneself poor, vile, abject, and unworthy of appearing in the presence of God. That celebrated expression among the ancients, *Know thyself*, while it refers to the knowledge of the grandeur and excellence of the soul, not to be degraded and profaned with things unworthy of its nobility, refers no less to the knowledge of our unworthiness, imperfection, and misery; inasmuch as the more miserable we recognize ourselves to be, the more we should confide in the goodness and mercy of God. For between mercy and misery there is a connection so close that one cannot be exercised without the other. If God had not created man, He would have truly been all good, but He would not have been actually merciful, because mercy is exercised only towards the miserable. You see then that the more miserable we know ourselves to be, the more occasion we have to confide in God, since we have nothing in ourselves in which to confide. Diffidence in ourselves proceeds from knowledge of our imperfections. It is very good to diffide[1] in ourselves, but what will it avail, unless we cast all our confidence on God, and expect His mercy?

Do you know that you are a poor little creature? Love to be such, glory in not being anything; be quite at ease, since your misery will serve as an object for the goodness of God to exercise His mercy upon.

Among the poor, those who are the most miserable, and whose maladies are greatest and most affecting, are considered the luckiest of the poor, and the most proper to obtain alms. We are only beggars, the most miserable are in the best condition, and the mercy of God regards them the more willingly.

Let us humble ourselves, I beseech you, and preach only our sores at the gate of the temple of divine piety. But remember to preach them with joy, consoling yourself to be all emptiness, that God may fill you with His kingdom. Be sweet and affable with everyone, except with

---

1   Diffide—to practice diffidence; to trust not in one's own strength (but to confide greatly, to have great confidence, in God).—*Publisher, 2013.*

those who would wish to take away your glory, which is your misery. "I glory in my infirmities," says the Apostle. (*2 Cor.* 12:9). And: "It is more advantageous for me to die" (*Phil.* 1:21) than to lose my glory. Do you see? He preferred to die rather than lose his infirmities, which were his glory.[2] You must guard well your misery, your baseness, for God regards it as He regarded that of the Sacred Virgin. (*Luke* 1:48). "Men behold the exterior, but God beholds the heart." (*1 Kings* 16:7). If He sees humility in our soul, He will bestow great graces upon us.

Let your heart then be full of courage, and your courage of confidence in God, for He who gave you the first attractions of His love will never abandon you, if you do not abandon Him: which I beseech you, with all my heart, not to do.

---

2 "God does not raise unjust reflections. Even when He shows us our faults, He represents them to us with sweetness; He condemns and consoles us at the same time, He humbles without troubling us, and turns us against ourselves in such a manner that, while confused at our misery, we are replenished with peace. The Lord is not in the whirlwind."—*Fenelon.*

CHAPTER FOUR

GOD HAS GIVEN US EVERYTHING WITH HIS DIVINE SON

G REAT indeed was the gift which the Eternal Father made to the world, when He bestowed upon it His own Son, as Our Lord Himself says: "God so loved the world, that He gave it His only begotten Son." How then (says the great Apostle St. Paul) has He not given us every other gift with Him?

You remember well, I am sure, the beautiful history of the holy patriarch Joseph, which has already been so often told, but which can never be too much considered: being viceroy of Egypt, his brothers, who dwelt in Mesopotamia, came suppliantly to him, in order to be assisted by him, in the extreme necessity to which their good father Jacob and they had been reduced, in consequence of the famine which desolated their country; you know also how kindly he sent them back to their father laden with wheat. But when they brought him little Benjamin, he sent them back, not as on the previous occasion, laden with grain and provisions given only by measure, but also accompanied them with the richest gifts, and with wagons filled with all they could desire. In the same manner, we see the Eternal Father acts towards us; for although, in the Old Law, He made very great presents to His people, yet they were always made by measure; on the contrary, in the New Law, from the moment of beholding His dear Benjamin, that is to say, Our Lord, re-enter into His glory, He has opened His most liberal hand to pour forth His gifts and graces on all the faithful most abundantly, as He had said by the prophet Joel: that He would pour out His Holy Spirit on all flesh, that is to say, on all men, and not merely on the Apostles.

Besides, you know what Isaias says of Our Lord, that He should[1] receive infinite graces, and that the gifts of the Holy Spirit would rest upon His head. "And the Spirit of the Lord," he says, "will rest upon him, the Spirit of wisdom and understanding, the Spirit of counsel and fortitude, the Spirit of knowledge and piety, and he shall be filled with the fear of the Lord." But why does the prophet say that all these gifts would rest upon Our Lord, since He neither had nor could have any need for them, being the very source of grace Himself? Merely to make us understand that all graces and celestial benedictions should be distributed by Him who is our head, allowing them to flow down on us who are His members, I mean to say, children of the holy

---

1   Should receive infinite graces—that is, *would* receive infinite graces. This archaic use of the word *should* occurs frequently in this text.—*Publisher*, 2013.

Church, of which He is the Head; and in proof of this truth, hear what He says in the Canticle of Canticles to His beloved: "Open to Me, My spouse, My sister." He calls her spouse, on account of the greatness of His love, and sister, to testify the purity and sincerity of this love. Open to Me, He says to her, but open to Me quickly; for My head is full of dew, and My locks of the drops of the night. Now, the dew and the drops of the night are but one and the same thing. What do you think, then, does this Well-beloved of our souls mean to say, unless that He ardently desires His beloved to open the door of her heart quickly to Him, in order that He may be able to pour out His sacred gifts and the graces which He has received most abundantly from His Eternal Father, as a dew and most precious liquor, of which He wishes to make her a present?

It is a thing most certain, and one which ought to console us greatly, that Jesus Christ, Our Lord and Master, in all the rigor of justice, and with a just price, paid and made satisfaction to God His Father for all the punishment that we have merited by our sins, and not only for all ours, but for all those of the whole world. This is what the great Doctor of the Gentiles declares to the Romans, saying that where sin had abounded, grace superabounded; he had there, he meant to say, sins in abundance, but graces in superabundance, and by grace we are to understand satisfaction.

Our Saviour, seeing that the Divine Majesty of His Father had the interests of human nature extremely at heart, without inquiring of the price, or of any other thing, at the very first, in order to redeem us, presented, with a most pure and liberal affection, a ransom which neither we nor the angels could procure, a satisfaction much greater than all that the sins of the world could require; whence St. Paul says: "You are bought with a great price;" the price indeed is great, and in harmony with the excellence of the thing. A great deposit was that, by which Our Lord lodged in the hands of the paternal Justice, all His Precious Blood, of which the least drop is far more valuable than all the worlds we could ever imagine.

It is no wonder, then, that Our Lord, having made such a payment, should destroy the decree by which we were delivered over to the hands of the devil, remarks the great Apostle.

But, I beg of you, listen for a little to the theological reason of this. Satisfaction is so much the greater and more valuable as the person who makes it is great, distinguished, and of more merit. Example: if I have received an injury from a prince, and he sends me a foot-boy in order to be reconciled with me and to make me satisfaction, this is not a great honor; but if he sends me his own son, who makes me satisfaction, and begs me to be no longer offended, this is a great honor, this satisfaction is greater than the injury could have been. And, in truth, how is satisfaction to be made for honor, unless by rendering honor? But honor is greater in proportion as he who renders it is more exalted; for the least honor that a prince renders is worth incomparably more than all the honors that a man of low condition could render: so much does honor depend on him who gives it.

Let us then say: if honor is so much the greater as he

who renders it is the more dignified, if satisfaction is so much the greater as he who makes it is the more exalted, what must be the satisfaction of Him who is infinitely great? The honor rendered and the satisfaction made by a personage of infinite perfection cannot but be infinite. Let us now see where we are. Our Lord was an infinite being; He satisfied for us, His satisfaction was infinite. Oh, then! How well could David say: In Our Lord there is great mercy, and a satisfaction ample and excellent! God, truly infinite, had been offended; Jesus Christ, truly infinite, satisfied; man had been elevated by pride against God Himself, Our Lord was humbled under every creature.

Understand this well; being equal to His Father, He humbled and annihilated Himself, even unto death, which is nothing else than a kind of total privation, and therefore God His Father gave Him a name which is above all names, the name of Jesus, which signifies Saviour, as if He had said: He is justly Saviour, who, being infinite, has paid the debt in all its rigor, with an infinite satisfaction.

Chapter Five

The Love of Jesus in His Incarnation

T HE love of God is always inseparably united with the love of the neighbor, and accordingly as we love God, we likewise love our neighbor; hence, the love of Jesus Christ towards His Father being infinite, His love towards men is likewise infinite. To give some certain proofs of it:

From the moment of His holy conception, He loved us with a marvelous love of complacency; for His delights were to be with the children of men and to draw man to Him, becoming man Himself, in order that in His humanity we might be able to approach and see Him with our eyes in Heaven, and by faith, here on earth, in the divine Sacrament of the Eucharist. He loved us with a love of benevolence, giving His own divinity to man, in such a manner that man became God;[1] He united Himself to us

---

1 St. Francis de Sales speaks of the "divinization" that is brought about by Sanctifying Grace.—*Publisher,* 2013.

by an incomprehensible junction, in which He adhered and was pressed to our nature so powerfully, indissolubly, and indescribably, that never was anything so closely joined and pressed to humanity as is now the most holy divinity in the person of the Son of God. He poured Himself entirely into us, and, so to speak, dissolved His greatness in order to reduce it to our littleness: whence He is called the fountain of living water, the rain and dew of heaven. He annihilated Himself, St. Paul says, to arrive at our humanity, to replenish us with His divinity, to overwhelm us with His goodness, to elevate us to His dignity, and to bestow on us the divine existence of children of God: He who dwelt in Himself, wishing to dwell henceforward in us; He who was living during ages of ages in the bosom of His Eternal Father, desiring to be made mortal in the womb of His temporal Mother; He who had always been God, becoming man for eternity. Ah, how beautiful to look upon Him, a little infant for us! Certainly we ought with a hundred thousand times more contentment see this dear little Infant lying in the crib, than all the potentates of the world sitting on their thrones. This amiable condition of a little infant excites us to love Him confidently, and to confide ourselves lovingly to Him in whom we find all. His poverty and His silence in the manger tell us much greater things than any human eloquence could, and raise within our hearts many holy sentiments and affections—above all, a perfect renunciation of the goods and pomps of this world.

I do not find any other mystery which so happily blends tenderness with austerity, love with rigor, and sweetness with severity.

Let us remain at the feet of this Saviour, saying with the spouse in the Canticles: "I have found Him whom my soul loveth, I will hold Him, and will not let Him go." The Infant in the crib does not say a word, and His heart, full of ardor for ours, is manifested only by sighs, tears, and sweet glances; but what great things does this silence say to me!

It teaches me to make true mental prayer; it shows me the loving fervor of a heart full of good thoughts, of holy affections: a heart that is afraid to lose their sweetness by expressing them.[2]

During His mortal life, the sweet Jesus never heaved a single sigh towards His Father, in which we had not a share, or entertained a single thought, which was not for our happiness. Though we were iron through hardness, or straw through weakness, we ought to love Him; He is a divine magnet that attracts iron, a celestial amber that attracts straw; in a word, He is the center of all hearts.

Pronounce often from the depth of your heart the sacred name of the Saviour: it will shed a delicious balm through all the powers of your soul. How happy we should be to have nothing in the understanding but Jesus, in the will but Jesus, in the imagination but Jesus! Let us try and pronounce it often and devoutly. May this divine Infant be pleased to bathe our hearts in His blood and to anoint

---

2   "Why, then, be afraid? O man, why dread so much the face of God? Is it because He comes? He comes indeed; but it is to save, not to judge, the earth. And that you may not have reason to say as formerly: *I heard Thy voice and hid myself;* here He has become an infant, and without a voice; for the wailings of infancy inspire less of fear than of compassion. He has become, I say, a little infant; a virgin, His mother, binds His tender limbs, and will you still be afraid? And even if a little infant should be feared, a little would suffice to appease it; for everyone knows that an infant is easily satisfied."—*St. Bernard.*

them with His holy name, in order that the good desires which we conceive may be all purpled and perfumed therewith! Let us a thousand times kiss the feet of this Saviour, and say to Him: My heart, O my God, desires Thee, my eyes seek Thee out, I sigh for Thy countenance; that is, let us keep our eyes fixed on Jesus Christ to consider Him, our mouth ever ready to praise Him, our whole being athirst to be agreeable to Him.

CHAPTER SIX

THE LOVE OF JESUS IN HIS PASSION

THE Eternal Father so loved the world that He gave it His only Son, and the Son so loved the will of His Father, who desired the salvation of human nature, that, without taking into account the meanness or contemptibleness of the thing, He willingly offered a prodigious price for its ransom, namely, His blood, His toils, and His life.

Thus Our Saviour, through love, devoted Himself to the will of His Father and to the redemption of the world. He advanced in every mystery of His Passion, saying: O my Father, this loved human nature would be sufficiently redeemed by one of my tears, but that would not suffice for the reverence which I owe to Thy will and to my love. I wish, besides my agony in the Garden of Olives, to be scourged, to be crowned with thorns, to have my body reduced to ruins, and to become as a leper, without form or beauty.

Thus the sweet Jesus was scourged, crowned, condemned, mocked, and rejected as man, devoted, destined,
and dedicated to carry out and endure the opprobriums
and ignominies due in punishment to all sins, and He
served as a general sacrifice for sin, being made as it were an
anathema, separated from and abandoned by His Eternal
Father.

The Divine Saviour wished to die in the flames of
love, because of the infinite charity He bore towards us,
and by the force and power of love; that is to say, He
would die in love, by love, for love, and of love. This is
what He Himself says: "No one takes away My life, but
I lay it down of Myself, for I have power to lay it down
and to take it up again." And: "He was offered," says Isaias,
"because He wished it." His body being by right immortal
and impassible,[1] on account of the glory of His soul, He
rendered it, through love and by a miracle, mortal and pas-
sible. He wished, even after His death, to have His side
opened, that we might see the thoughts of His heart, which
were all thoughts of love, and that we might go to Him
with confidence, in order to hide ourselves in His side, and
to receive from Him an abundance of graces and benedictions. In this manner, from the first moment of His life
until the present hour, has the kind Jesus been continually
drawing arrows, if we may so speak, from the quiver of His
love, with which to wound the souls of His lovers, showing
them clearly that they can never love Him near so much as
He deserves. My God, could He show more love to sinners

---

1   Impassible—unable to suffer.—*Publisher,* 2013.

than to become a perfect holocaust for their sins? Ah! If we could see the Heart of Jesus such as it is, we should die of love for Him, since we are mortal, as He died of love for us, while He was mortal, and as He would die again, if He were not now immortal. Nothing has so much power to wound a loving heart as to see another heart wounded for love of it. Oh! That Our Lord would change hearts with us, as He did with St. Catherine of Siena, in such a manner that we might have no other heart but His, no other will but His, no other affection or desire but to love Him and to be wholly His.

The pelican, seeing its little one stung by serpents, wounds them on all sides with the point of its bill, in order that the venom imparted to the body by the serpents may be extracted with their blood, but seeing them die, it wounds itself, and pours out its blood upon them, as if to vivify them with a new life. Its love wounds them, and suddenly, through this same love, it wounds itself. Bees never wound without being wounded to death.

Seeing, then, the Saviour of our souls wounded with love for us, even to death and the death of the cross, shall not we be wounded with love for Him, and with a wound most lovingly dolorous? Never, indeed, can we love Him so much as His love and His death deserve.

Ah! If my soul is the spouse of Jesus crucified and suffering, I ought, during my whole life, to regard it as a great favor to wear His livery, that is to say, the nails, the thorns, and the lance. Remember, my soul, that the banquet of His nuptials is prepared of gall and vinegar; seek not for pleasure or joy in this world. It is too great an honor, O King of Glory, to drink with Thee the chalice of sorrow; may it never happen to me to refuse this draught, because, O God, says David, it is the beverage of thy beloved!

The image of Jesus Christ bruised, wounded, pierced, crushed, crucified, has always been a beautiful mirror of love, into which the angels and saints could never cease to gaze, enraptured with sweetness and overflowing with consolation. And if the picture of Abraham, wielding the sword of death over his dear and only son, had power to make the great St. Gregory, Bishop of Nyssa, weep as often as he contemplated it, how much more ought the image of Our Lord, sacrificing Himself on the cross, to move us: a sacrifice which is the source of all the graces we have ever received, and of all our holy resolutions, in such a manner that through it alone we preserve, fortify, and accomplish them?

Since, then, Our Lord has so much loved us, that He has equally redeemed all, bedewed us with His divine blood, and called us to Himself, without excluding anyone; since He has become all ours, to make us all His, giving us His death and His life to deliver us from eternal death and to procure us the joys of eternal life, that we may belong to Him in this mortal life and yet more perfectly in the next; what remains, what conclusion have we to draw, unless that living we should no longer live for ourselves, but for Jesus Christ who died for us; that is, we should consecrate to Him every moment of our life, referring to His glory our works, our thoughts, and our affections?

My soul, live henceforward amid the scourges and the thorns of thy Saviour, and there, as a nightingale in its bush, sing sweetly: Live Jesus, who didst die that my soul might live! Ah, Eternal Father! What can the world return Thee for the present Thou hast made it of Thy only Son? Alas! To redeem a thing so vile as I, the Saviour delivered Himself to death, and, unhappy me! I hesitate to surrender my nothingness to Him who has given me everything.

Chapter Seven

Abundance of Our Redemption

GOD clearly foresaw that the first man would abuse his liberty, and that forsaking grace he would lose glory, but He did not wish to treat human nature so rigorously as He decreed to treat the angelic.

It was of human nature He had determined to take a blessed piece, to unite it to His divinity. He saw that it was a feeble nature, *a wind which passeth and returneth not,* that is to say, which is dissipated as it goes. He had regard to the surprise of the assault which the malicious and perverse Satan made on the first man, and to the greatness of the temptation which ruined him. He saw that the whole race of men would perish by the fault of a single one. For these reasons, He looked upon our nature in pity, and resolved to receive it to mercy.

The devil had taken us away from our natural Lord, and though he had no title to us, yet Our Lord redeemed us, redeemed what was His own, to make us more His own, if more His own we could be. St. Paul says: "You are bought with a great price." What is this price? *He redeemed us with the blood of the Lamb;* He pardoned not His own Son, but delivered Him to death for us.

That the sweetness of His mercy might be adorned by the beauty of His justice, He resolved to save man by means of a rigorous redemption, which no one being able to make except His own Son, He appointed that He should redeem men, not merely by one of His loving actions, which would have been more than sufficient to redeem a thousand millions of worlds, but by all the innumerable loving actions and dolorous sufferings He would perform and endure even to death, and the death of the cross, to which He destined Him: wishing that thus He should become the companion of our miseries in order to make us the companions of His glory hereafter, showing in this manner the riches of His goodness by a *redemption copious,* abundant, magnificent, and excessive, which acquired, and, as it were, reconquered for us all the means necessary to attain to glory; so that no person can ever complain as if the divine mercy were wanting to him.

The least drop of Our Lord's blood was of infinitely more value than we, and nevertheless, to make us more His own, He wished to shed it all.

Who will doubt the abundance of our means of salvation, since we have so great a Saviour, in consideration of whom we have been created, and by the merits of whom we have been redeemed? For He died for all, because all were dead, and His mercy has been more salutary to redeem the race of man, than the misfortune of Adam was venomous to destroy. And so far from the sin of Adam having exceeded, it has, on the contrary, rather excited, the Divine Goodness, which, by a sweet and loving contention, being invigorated by the presence of its adversary, and massing, as it were, all its forces for victory, has made *grace superabound where iniquity had abounded;* so that holy Church, in an excess of admiration, cries out on the eve of Easter: "O truly necessary sin of Adam, which has been blotted out by the death of Jesus Christ! O happy fault, which merited such and so great a Redeemer!" Certainly we can say with one of the ancients: we were lost, if we had not been lost; that is to say, our loss has been to our gain, since, in fact, human nature has received more graces by the redemption of its Saviour, than it would ever have received by the innocence of Adam, if he had persevered in it.

Though the Divine Providence has left in man, along with the grace of its mercy, several striking marks of its severity, such as, for example, the necessity of death, the pains of sickness, the obligation of labor, the rebellion of sensuality, yet the celestial clemency, rising above these, takes pleasure in turning every misery to the greater advantage of those who love it, making patience spring up from labor, contempt of the world from the necessity of death, and a thousand victories from concupiscence; and, as the rainbow touching the thorny aspalathus renders it more odorous than the lily,[1] so the redemption of Our Lord touching our miseries renders them more useful

---

1   St. Francis often compares spiritual realities to the things of nature. Many of these natural phenomena seem to be drawn from folklore rather than from the serious sciences, even those of his day; nevertheless, the points that are made by means of the comparisons remain valid.—*Publisher,* 2013.

and more amiable than original innocence would ever have been.

"The angels have more joy in Heaven," says the Saviour, "for one sinner that does penance, than for ninety-nine just who need not penance." And in like manner, the state of redemption is a hundred times better than that of innocence. Through the sprinkling of the blood of Our Lord, made with the hyssop of the cross, we have been restored to a whiteness incomparably more excellent than that of the snow of innocence: coming forth, like Naaman, from the river of salvation, purer and cleaner than if we had never been defiled, in order that the Divine Majesty *might not be overcome by evil, but might overcome evil with good,* and that His mercies might be exalted *over all His works.*

Chapter Eight

Our Lord Practiced All the Most Excellent Kinds of Love

1. HE LOVED us with a love of complacency, for *His delights were to be with the children of men,* and to draw man to Him, becoming man Himself.

2. He loved us with a love of benevolence, pouring His own divinity into man, in such a manner that man was made God.

3. He united Himself to us by a union so close and incomprehensible, that nothing was ever so closely united as the most holy divinity and humanity are now in the person of Our Lord.

4. He dissolved, as it were, His greatness, to reduce it to the form and figure of our littleness; whence He is called the fountain of living water, the rain and dew of heaven.

5. He fell into ecstasy,[1] not only, as St. Denis says,

---

1 St. Francis is referring to the root meaning of the word *ecstasy:* "to be outside of (oneself)."—*Publisher,* 2013.

because, through the excess of His loving goodness, He became in a manner out of Himself, extending His Providence to all things, and finding Himself in all; but also because, as St. Paul says, He quitted Himself, emptied Himself, laid aside His glory and grandeur, descended from the throne of His incomprehensible majesty, and, so to speak, *annihilated Himself,* in order to arrive at our humanity, to replenish us with His divinity, to overwhelm us with His goodness, to elevate us to His dignity, and to bestow on us the divine existence of children of God; and that expression which has been so often used: "I live," saith the Lord, He has been able to repeat in the language of His Apostle: "I live, now not I, but *man* liveth in Me; My life is *man,* and to die for *man* is My gain; My life is hidden with *man* in God." He who dwelt in Himself wishes henceforward to dwell in us; He who had lived from unbeginning ages in the bosom of His Eternal Father becomes mortal in the womb of His temporal Mother; He who had eternally been God becomes Man for eternity; to such a degree has God been ravished and drawn into an ecstasy, through love for man.

6. He loved us to admiration, as shown in the cases of the Centurion and the Canaanite woman.

7. He lovingly contemplated the young man who had observed the commandments from his youth, and desired to know the way to perfection.

8. He took a loving rest among us, and sometimes with suspension of the senses, as in the womb of His Mother, and during His infancy.

9. He had tendernesses towards little children whom

He took in His arms and lovingly caressed, towards Martha and Magdalen, towards Lazarus over whom He wept, as also over the city of Jerusalem.

10. He was animated with an extraordinary zeal, which, as St. Denis says, made Him jealous: turning away, as far as lay in Him, all evil from His loved human nature, even at the risk and peril of His own life; banishing the devil, the prince of this world, who appeared as His rival and competitor.

11. He had a thousand thousand loving languors; from which proceeded those divine words: "I have a baptism wherewith I am to be baptized, and how I am straitened until it be accomplished!" He foresaw the hour of being baptized in His own blood, and languished for its arrival, the love He bore us pressing Him to see us delivered by His death from eternal death. Thus He was sorrowful even to a bloody sweat in the Garden of Olives, not only through the bitter grief He felt in the inferior part of His soul, but also through the immense love He bore us in the rational part: the one giving Him a horror of death, the other an extreme desire of it: so that between this horror and this desire He suffered a most cruel agony, even to a great *effusion of blood*, which flowed as from a fountain, *trickling down upon the ground.*

12. Finally, this Divine Lover died in the midst of the flames of holy love, because of the infinite charity He bore towards us, and by the force and efficacy of love, that is to say, He died in love, by love, for love, and of love. For, though the cruel torments were more than sufficient to cause the death of anyone, yet death could not enter into

the life of Him who *held the keys of life and death,* unless Divine Love had first opened the gates to death, allowing it to enter and to plunder His divine body of life; love not being content with having made Him mortal for us, if it did not also see Him die. It was by election, and not by compulsion, that He died. "No one taketh away My life," He says, "but I lay it down of Myself; I have power to lay it down, and to take it up again." "He was offered," says Isaias, "because He willed it;" and therefore it is not said that His spirit departed, or separated itself from Him, but on the contrary that He gave up His spirit, breathed it out, and placed it in the hands of His Eternal Father. Accordingly, St. Athanasius remarks that He *bowed down His head* to die, thereby to consent to the approach of death, which otherwise could not dare touch Him; and, *crying out with a loud voice,* He surrendered His spirit to His Father, to show that as He had sufficient strength and breath not to die, yet He had so much love that He could no longer live without vivifying by His death those who otherwise could never avoid death, or attain to true life. On this account, the death of the Saviour was a true sacrifice, and a holocaustic sacrifice, which He Himself offered to His Father, for our redemption. While the pains and dolors of His Passion were so great and excessive that any other person would have died of them, yet, as far as regarded Him, He never would have died of them if He had not willed it, or if the fire of His infinite charity had not consumed His life. He was then the High Priest who offered Himself to His Father, and He immolated Himself in love, to love, by love, for love, and of love.

Beware, however, of thinking that this loving death of the Saviour happened after the manner of a rapture. The object for which His charity led Him to death was not so amiable as to ravish His divine soul to it. No, His soul quitted His body after the manner of an ecstasy, pushed and impelled by love, as we see myrrh pouring out its first liquor from abundance alone, without being pressed or drawn in any way. This accords with what He Himself has said, as already remarked: "No one takes away or ravishes my life from Me, but I lay it down voluntarily." O God, what a furnace to inflame us to the performance of the exercises of holy love for a Saviour so good, seeing that He so lovingly performed them for us who are so bad! The sweet *charity of Jesus Christ presses us!*

CHAPTER NINE

GOD LOOKS UPON US LOVINGLY, NOTWITHSTANDING OUR WEAKNESS

YOU ask me whether Our Lord thinks of you, and whether He looks upon you with love. Yes, He thinks of you, and not only of you, but of the least hair of your head. This is an article of faith. We cannot doubt it. I know well indeed that you do not doubt it, but only express, as you have done the dryness, aridity, and insensibility in which you at present find your soul. "Truly God is in this place, and I knew it not," said Jacob; that is to say, I had no sentiment of it, it did not appear so to me.

And that God looks upon you with love you have no reason to doubt, for He looks upon the most dreadful sinners in the world lovingly when they have the least true desire to be converted to Him. Tell me, do you not intend to belong to God? Do you not desire to serve Him faithfully? And who gave you this desire, this intention, unless Himself in His loving regard for you?

To examine whether your heart pleases Him is not necessary, but rather whether His Heart pleases you. And if you look upon His Heart, it is impossible but that it will please you, for it is a Heart most sweet, most kind, most condescending, most gracious towards miserable creatures, provided that they acknowledge their misery. And who will not love this royal Heart, so full of tenderness for us?

You remark very well that these temptations happen to you because your heart is without tenderness towards God; for it is quite true that if you had tenderness, you would have consolation, and if you had consolation, you would no longer be in pain. But the love of God does not consist in consolation nor in tenderness, for if it did, then Our Lord would not have loved His Father when He was sad even to death and cried out: "My Father, My Father, why hast Thou abandoned me?" And still it was at that moment He made the greatest act of love which it is possible to conceive.

We would always like to have a little consolation, a little sugar in our tea, that is to say, the feeling of love and tenderness, and consequently consolation; and in like manner we would much wish to be without imperfections; but we must have patience to belong to human nature, and not to angelic nature. Our imperfections ought not to please us; on the contrary, we should say with the holy Apostle: "Oh, miserable me! Who will deliver me from this body of death?" But they ought not to astonish us, or to take away our courage; we ought even to derive submission, humility, and distrust of ourselves from them, but not discouragement, nor affliction of heart, much less doubt-fulness of God's love towards us. Thus, as the weakness and infirmity of a child displease its mother, yet she does not cease to love it, but cherishes it with tenderness and compassion, so God, while He approves not of our imperfections and venial sins, does not cease to love us tenderly; hence David had reason to say to God: "Have pity on me, O Lord, for I am weak."

But enough! Live joyful; Our Lord looks upon you with love, and with so much the more tenderness as you are the more feeble. Never permit your mind willingly to entertain thoughts to the contrary; and when they come, regard them not, turn your eyes away from their iniquity, and have recourse to God with a courageous humility, to speak to Him of His ineffable goodness by which He loves us, poor, abject, and miserable as we are.

Alas! What obligations we are under to Our Lord, and how much confidence we should have that what His mercy has begun in us it will accomplish, and that He will give such increase to this little vessel of oil, the good will we have, that all our vessels will be filled with it, and many others belonging to our neighbors too! But we must close the door of our chamber fast, that is, retire along with our heart more and more into the Divine Goodness.

Chapter Ten

How Much Our Sweet Saviour Loved Every One of Us Personally

CONSIDER the love with which Jesus Christ Our Lord suffered so much in this world, particularly in the Garden of Olives, and on Mount Calvary. His love had you in view, and by a long series of pains and sufferings obtained from God the Father the good resolutions of your heart, and whatever else was necessary for you in order to nourish and strengthen them. O resolutions, how precious you are, since you are the fruit of the Passion of my Saviour! How much my soul ought to cherish you, since you are so dear to my Jesus! O Saviour of my soul, you would die in order to purchase these resolutions for me: grant that I may die rather than lose them!

Think well on it, faithful soul: it is certain that on the tree of the cross the Heart of our Lord Jesus beheld yours, and that He loved it, and by His love obtained for it all the favors which you have ever received, or will ever receive: among them, your good resolutions. Yes, pious soul, we can all say with Jeremias: "O Lord, before I existed Thou hadst regard to me, and didst call me by name."

What a difference between those who enjoy the light of the sun, and those who have only the faint light of a lamp! The former are not jealous or envious of one another, for they well know that their light is more than sufficient for all, that its enjoyment by one does not hinder its enjoyment by another, and that no one possesses it less while all possess it in common. But as for the light of a lamp, which is feeble, of brief duration, and insufficient for many, everyone desires to have it in his own chamber, and here arises an occasion of dissension. The worth of sublunary things is so contemptible and mean, that while one enjoys them it is necessary that another should be deprived of them; and human friendship is so uncertain and weak that in proportion as it is communicated towards some it is enfeebled towards others; on which account we are jealous and annoyed when we have not companions. The Heart of God is so abundant in love, its excellence is so infinitely great, that all can possess it without anyone possessing it less, this infinity never being exhausted, though all the beings in the universe should be filled with it; for after all are filled, its infinity always remains the same, without any diminution. The sun does not look less upon one rose in the midst of a thousand millions of other flowers than if he looked down upon it alone. And God does not shed His love less upon one soul while He loves an infinity of others than if He loved it alone, the force of His love not being diminished by the multitude of rays which it sends forth, but remaining full of His immensity.

Ah, my God! How frequently we should put the query to our soul: Is it possible that I have been loved, and so tenderly loved by my Saviour, that He was pleased to think of me in particular, and in all those little occurrences by which He has drawn me to Him? How much should we appreciate them, and how carefully turn them to our profit!

What is sweeter than this thought: the amiable Heart of my God thought of my soul, loved it, and procured a thousand means of salvation for it, as if He had no other soul to think of in the world? As the sun enlightening one portion of the earth, shines nothing less than if it did not shine there, so Our Lord thought of and labored for all His dear children in such a way, that He thought of every one of them as if He never had a thought of the others. "He loved me," says St. Paul, "and delivered Himself for me;" as if to say: for me alone, and just the same as if He had done nothing for the rest of men. This consideration, faithful soul, should be engraven on your heart, to nourish and strengthen your resolutions, which are so dear to the Saviour.

God, then, is good to you; is it not true? But to whom is the supreme lover of hearts not good? Those who taste Him can never be satiated, and those who approach His Heart cannot refrain from praising and blessing Him forever.

After having made these touching considerations, you ought often to repeat with heart and mouth the burning words of St. Paul, St. Augustine, St. Catherine of Siena, and others: "No, I am no longer mine; whether I live or die, I belong to my Saviour."

There is nothing left of me or mine; my being is Jesus, my property to belong to Him. O world, thou art always the same, and I indeed have always been myself. No, we shall no longer be ourselves, for our hearts will be changed, and the world, which has so often deceived us, will be deceived by us; for, perceiving our change only by little and little, it will imagine us to be Esaus, and we shall really be Jacobs.

It is necessary that all these sentiments should sink deep into our hearts, and that, leaving our reflections and our prayers, we should pass to our affairs sweetly, lest the liquor of our good resolutions should evaporate and be lost; for we must allow it to saturate and penetrate our whole soul: everything, nevertheless, without strain of mind or body.

CHAPTER ELEVEN

LOVE OF JESUS FOR SINNERS

OUR Lord, the great and excellent physician of our
infirmities, announced everywhere, before coming into this world, both His arrival and the maladies He
would cure; sometimes by His prophets: "I will bind up
that which was broken and I will comfort that which was
weak. The Spirit of the Lord is upon Me; to teach the poor
He hath sent Me, to heal the contrite of heart. They will be
cleansed from all their iniquities—and Thou shalt save the
humble;" sometimes by His own mouth: "Come to Me,
all ye that are weary;" but, above all, when He was called
Jesus, for physicians do not always cure, and therefore it
was not sufficient to call Him merely physician, but He
should be called *Saviour,* inasmuch as His remedies are
infallible. What wonder then if in the Gospel we find Him
surrounded by the sick, by sinners, and by publicans! O
vain and foolish murmuring of the Jews, when they said:

"This man receiveth sinners." Whom would you wish Him to receive? Is it not the honor of a physician to be sought for by the sick, and so much the more as their maladies are considered incurable? Our Lord, not so much to condemn the temerity of these Pharisees as to give us courage to approach Him, banished far from Him, by fitting similitudes, their ungrounded supposition. Let us conclude then with reason from His discourse, that it is His pleasure to lead back sinners to mercy.[1]

The soul departs from God, flying away from His graces and the means which He proposes for our salvation, as we say that a man flies from physicians: not that he hates the person so much as the prescription of the physician.

By how far sinners are from God, by so far are they from His mercies. What a pity! What regrets! For that which the great St. Augustine says is most true: "Lord, Thou hast made us for Thyself, and our heart cannot rest, but in Thee." Oh! What disorder in man with regard to his God and with regard to himself! But there is one consolation in the midst of so great a desolation, that, though the sinner is far from God, he may return and will be well received. "Let the impious forsake his way, and the wicked man his thoughts, and let him return to the Lord, and He will have pity on him; for He is bounteous in His mercy to

---

1   "Though it may happen that a mother should be so hardened as to forget her child, yet God promises He will never forget us. His mercy is so great that He is always ready to pardon anyone who wishes to return to his duty. The Divine Goodness and the truly penitent soul are so well in accordance that, after reconciliation, there does not appear one trace of a rupture having taken place; the Divine Goodness does not reproach the soul for its past irregularities but arranges everything so happily that past irregularities are never of any prejudice to the soul that has resolved to correct them."—*Thaulerus.*

forgive."[2] Thus, how were the poor Prodigal and the unfortunate Absalom received by their fathers? And, otherwise, what would become of us, for *all have sinned*? *Every man is a liar*, that is to say, a sinner. If we say that we are without sin, we deceive ourselves. *Return to the Lord, and forsake your injustice; for His mercy is great towards those who are converted to Him.* Why is He called Saviour, unless in order to save? *Sinners and publicans drew nigh to hear His word.*[3]

In the twenty-second chapter of the First Book of Kings, it is related of David, that being in the cave of Odollam, needy and afflicted men gathered to him, and he became their king; this was to prefigure the second and true David, who should allow the poor and needy, the afflicted and the miserable, those groaning under the heavy burden of corporal infirmities, and much more those sinking under the insupportable burden of sin, to approach to Him.

The Pharisees murmur because He receives sinners; but let us observe for a little how He receives them, and

---

2   Observe that God not only says He will pardon the ordinary sinner, one who has been carried away by common passions, but even the impious, that is to say, the man without faith, without law, without religion, the man who has insolently risen up against God and His Christ, who has uttered a thousand blasphemies, who has outraged Heaven and scandalized earth by the frightful impiety of his language, who, even as a Manasses, has destroyed the worship of God, overthrown its altars, erected idols in their place. This is the monster, the very thought of whom makes us tremble, that God promises to forgive, not after a long lapse of years, spent in laborious penance, but on the very first day of his conversion, though it should be the last of his life, if his return to God is sincere. And you, souls of little faith, still doubt whether God pardons you your old wanderings, although for a long time you have wept over, or at least detested, them.

3   We can say that there is nothing more in conformity with the inclinations of Jesus than to succor the miserable and to show mercy to those who ask pardon for their offences. Let no person then fear to implore His mercy, and let everyone know the difference that St. Bernard draws between the elect and the reprobate: the latter, he says, think not of rising after their fall, but the former no sooner fall than they rise again and are only the more ready to run in the way of God.

we shall behold great wonders. That the sinner can depart from God, and from himself, is certain. The Spirit goeth and returneth not. "Thy destruction is thine own, O Israel; thy help is only in Me." And St. Paul: "We are not capable of ourselves to have any good thought, but our sufficiency is from God." We can run away quickly enough, but cannot make one step back again. Our Lord prevents[4] the sinner and goes to seek him, calls him and invites him to return; otherwise, the sinner would never think of it. *I acknowledge that my strength comes from Thee, my God, because Thou art my support. The mercy of my God will prevent me.* It is God who produces good wishes and desires within us, and it is He who perfects them, and conducts them to execution. *Draw me after thee, and we shall run.* He who voyages with the wind, returns with a contrary wind. Never would Absalom have returned to his father, if the Thecuan woman had not obtained his forgiveness; never would the sinner return, if mercy did not prevent him. O infinite goodness! Our Lord goes in search of the lost sheep; otherwise, it would never return. Ah! Though some murmur at mercy, let us at least praise it, for it receives sinners, and seeks them. Jesus being in the temple on the day of the great solemnity, cries out, saying: "If anyone thirst, let him come to Me and drink; come to Me all you, etc. The Son of Man is come to seek and save that which was lost. How many times would I have gathered them together as the hen gathereth her chickens!"[5]

---

4   Prevents the sinner—that is, *goes before* the sinner (from the Latin *prae* and *venire*), anticipating and prompting his repentance by His graces.—*Publisher,* 2013.

5   God has promised to pardon, and to pardon the greatest and most numerous crimes. "Yes," He says by His prophet, "though your sins should have made your soul as red

But, oh, miserable that we are! We are often called, and we only turn a deaf ear. "I have called, and you have not heard," says God. We are drawn, and we obstinately resist Him. He complains, saying: "All the day long have I stretched out My hands to this incredulous and rebellious people."

O holy, fortunate, and happy crowd of sinners and publicans, who approach to Our Lord! They are not like those invited to the great feast, who excused themselves: they come, and are welcome. O my Saviour, how have these sinners drawn nigh to Thee, since Thou art just? For David says absolutely of the just man that evil must not approach to him: "Depart from Me, ye wicked." "No one can come to Me, unless My Father draw him; and him who cometh to Me I will not cast forth." Since it is thus, O Saviour, O Redeemer, O good God, I can say to the multitude on Thy part: "Approach to God, and you will be enlightened, and your faces will not be confounded; for He receives sinners."

But behold the manner of approaching to Him: we must retire from sin. "Retire from evil. Go out from Babylon, flee the Chaldees; peace is not with the wicked," says the Lord. You have sinned by thought, word, and deed; you must have recourse to contrary things, contrition, confession, and satisfaction.

---

as scarlet, I will make it as white as snow. You are plunged in crime, and it is only with horror I behold you. Still I cannot turn away My eyes from you, and close My ears to your prayers. Be converted, change your thoughts, desires, and conduct, cease to do evil, learn to do good, and then come before Me with confidence, and if I do not hear you, accuse Me as unfaithful to My promises." We can then, with the just Israelite, tell God to remember His promises and to keep His word by pardoning our sins: a word which supports our hope in the remembrance of our crimes, and without which we should fall into despair.

Our Lord is like the sun which shines everywhere. "His course is from the summit of Heaven." He sheds his rays on the just and the unjust, and from the muddiest pools extracts vapors, which, arrived at a certain elevation, are converted into a gentle rain, which, falling in its turn, gives life and fruitfulness to plants. From the greatest sinners, God brings forth holy exhalations, which are considerations on their faults, up to a certain height of fear and apprehension, as to a middle region of the air; considering that they are between Heaven and Hell, between salvation and damnation. "His spirit breathes, and the waters flow." These are the waters of contrition, which make the earth germinate and produce the fruits of salvation. But we must allow ourselves to be drawn, we must acknowledge our miserable condition. Let us then depart, let us depart from Egypt, let us approach Our Lord, let us make provision of good works; let the feet of our affections be bare, let us clothe ourselves with innocence, let us not be satisfied with crying for mercy, let us go forth from Egypt, let us delay no longer. The hour is come to arise from sleep, since we know that He receives sinners; the angels await our repentance, the saints pray for it.

Chapter Twelve

How Much the Mercy of God Appears in the Conversions of St. Paul and David

WHEN the Saviour came into the world, men had arrived at the height of malice. Among the Jews, the laws were in the hands of Annas and Caiphas, than whom none could be more wicked. Herod reigned in Galilee, Pontius Pilate presided in Judea. It was at this time, I say, that God came into the world to redeem us, and to deliver us from the slavery of sin and the tyranny of our enemy: impelled by His immense goodness alone to communicate Himself to us. Truly the Heart of our Divine Saviour and Master was all full of mercy and meekness towards the human race, and He gave many admirable proofs and testimonies of it on innumerable occasions when His mercy made His greatness shine forth, as we read in various portions of the Holy Scripture.

When was St. Paul forgiven, unless when he had arrived at the height of malice? Everyone knows that at the time of his conversion, he was in the midst of his greatest hatred and fury against God, and unable to satisfy his rage against our Saviour, had turned his wrath against the Church, which, if possible, he would have driven from the face of the earth; *breathing out threatenings and slaughter against the disciples of the Lord;* and, nevertheless, it was then that the Lord vanquished his malice and ingratitude, touched his heart, converted him, forgave all his iniquities, even at the very time when he was most undeserving of mercy. O God, how great was the divine mercy in regard to this holy Apostle! Yet we every day see like effects of the goodness of God towards sinners; for when they are most hardened in their sins, and have come to such a degree of malice that they live as if there were neither a God, nor a Heaven, nor a Hell, it is then He manifests the bowels of His pity and His sweet compassion, sending a ray of His divine light into their souls, discovering to them their miserable condition, that they may arise from it.

But never do I read of the conversion of David without being astonished to see that this prophet, after having committed such great sins, remained for nearly a year without returning to himself, buried in a profound lethargy, never awaking or perceiving his miserable condition. O God! His sin would have been in some manner excusable, if it had been committed whilst he was yet a shepherd, tending his flocks; but that David should have sinned after having received so many and such great graces from the Divine Majesty, so many lights and favors, after having wrought such marvels and prodigies, after having been brought up in the bosom of the sweet clemency and mercy of God; that he should have committed such crimes, and remained afterwards for so long a time without recognizing them, oh, this is indeed a matter of the greatest amazement!

He commits many sins, heaping them upon one another, and lies stagnating in his iniquities for nearly a year, without perceiving his miserable state or remembering his God!

Behold poor David then without any disposition for grace, through his forgetfulness of God; but the Divine Goodness, seeing his blindness, and to withdraw him from sin, sends him the prophet Nathan, who, wishing to make him recognize his fault, uses a parable: telling him that a rich man, who had a large number of sheep and oxen, had taken away from a poor man one single little lamb, which he had nourished in his house, and which he singularly loved. See, I beg of you, how wisely the prophet speaks to him in the third person of his fault, in order to make him recognize and confess it; but David, plunged in such complete blindness as not to see his sin, does not perceive that the prophet Nathan refers to him in any manner, and pronounces sentence of death against the man who had stolen the sheep, commanding him, moreover, to restore fourfold its value.

Consider, I beg of you, how hardened poor David was in his sin, of which he had not any sentiment; but as for the faults of others, he could very well be aware of them, and knew how to impose a punishment proportioned to their guilt. But the prophet Nathan, seeing that David did not recognize his sins, told him boldly that it was he who had stolen away the lamb, which poor David understanding, being struck with contrition, he cried out: "I have sinned against the Lord." *Peccavi Domino.* Then Nathan said to him: "Because you have confessed your sin, God forgives you, and you shall not die."

Now, what greater effect would you wish to see of the mercy of God than this? For, at the time when David would appear to have reached the very summit of his malice, God forgave his iniquity. But what a change did he manifest after recognizing his fault! He did nothing but weep and deplore his blindness; no other word was heard from him than this, *Peccavi,*[1] and, crying to God for mercy, he went about continually repeating the psalm of penance, *Miserere mei, Deus.*[2]

There are many other similar examples in the Holy Scriptures, by which God has displayed to us the greatness of His mercy, and from which we see the truth of these words of Isaias: "Because their malice has come to its height, it will be forgiven them."

---

1   *Peccavi*—"I have sinned."—*Publisher,* 2013.
2   *Miserere mei, Deus*—"Have mercy on me, [O] God."—*Publisher,* 2013.

CHAPTER THIRTEEN

HOW GREAT IS THE MERCY OF GOD ON THE RETURN OF THE SINNER[1]

THE entrance of sin takes away life from the heart and from all its good works; the entrance of grace restores life to the heart and to all its good works. A severe winter kills the plants of the field, so that, were it to continue always, they should remain forever dead. Sin, the sad and fearful winter of the soul, kills the holy works which it finds there, and, were it to continue always, never should life or vigor return. But as, on the approach of lovely spring, not

---

1   "There is not a page in the Gospel in which we do not see that Jesus has a certain tenderness for reconciled sinners more than for the just who persevere. Who does not know that the penitent Magdalen was His faithful and His well beloved; that Peter, after having denied Him, was chosen to confirm the faith of his brethren; that He left the whole flock in the desert to run after His lost sheep; and that the one of all His children who most sensibly moved His bowels [inmost being, heart], was the returned Prodigal? Hence we are to understand that while innocence has its tears, He esteems more precious those which sins cause to flow in the holy weepings of penance, and that justice recovered has something more agreeable in His eyes than justice preserved."—*Bossuet.*

only the new seeds which we cast into the earth, shoot up and bud, under the influence of this mild season of fecundity, every one according to its kind, but also the old plants, which the bitterness of the preceding winter had wasted and withered, grow green again, and take back their former life; so sin being destroyed, and the grace of Divine Love coming back to the soul, not only the new affections, which the return of the sacred springtime brings, germinate and produce many merits and benedictions, but also the works faded away under the harshness of the winter of past sin, being delivered from their mortal enemy, are reinvigorated, and, as it were, resuscitated, flourish anew, and fructify in merits for eternal life. Such is the omnipotence of celestial love, or rather the love of celestial omnipotence. "If the impious man turn away from his impiety, and do judgment and justice, his soul shall live. Be converted, and do penance for your iniquities, and your iniquity shall not be to your ruin," says the Almighty Lord. And what does He mean by saying: "Iniquity shall not be to your ruin," unless that the ruins it had made will be repaired? Thus, besides the thousand caresses which the Prodigal Son received from his father, he was re-established in all the dignities and advantages he had lost. And Job, an image of the penitent sinner, received in the end *double of all he had possessed*. God, then, does not forget the works of those who, having lost His holy love by sin, recover it by penance.[2] But God forgets

---

2   "We learn from the Saviour of souls that the conversion of sinful man is a feast to the heavenly spirits, our sighs are their joy, our grief their thanksgiving. The tears of penitents are so precious that they are received on earth to be carried to Heaven, and their efficacy is so great, that they reach even to the angels. And what is more wonderful is, that whilst innocence has its tears, the angels value more those which sins call forth;

works, when they lose their merit and sanctity by supervening sin, and only remembers them again when they return to life and value by the presence of love; so that the faithful, in order to be recompensed for their good works, as well by an increase of grace, as in the enjoyment of future glory and of eternal life, are not obliged never to relapse into sin, but it suffices, according to the sacred Council of Trent, to depart this life in the grace and charity[3] of God.

God has promised an eternal recompense to the works of the just man; but *if the just man turn away from his justice* by sin, God will no longer remember his justices, or the good works which he has done. But if, nevertheless, this poor man, after falling into sin, rises again, and returns to Divine Love by penance, God will no longer remember his sin, and if He will no longer remember his sin, He will then remember his preceding good works, and the recompense they had deserved, since sin, which alone can take them away from the divine memory, is effaced, abolished, and annihilated; thus the justice of God obliges His mercy, or rather, His mercy obliges His justice, to regard anew the past good works, as if they had never been forgotten; otherwise, the penitent king would not have dared to say to his Master: "Restore unto me the joy of Thy salvation;" and confirm me with Thy *perfect spirit.* For as you see, he not only seeks a *newness of spirit* and of heart, but asks that the

---

and the bitterness of penance has something sweeter in their eyes than the honey of devotion. Understand, O penitent sinners! That your tears penetrate the heavens, and rejoice the angels; see how fruitful they are to those who shed them, since they are prized by the celestial intelligences. What abundant satisfaction will affliction of heart one day produce in us, since it already effects such joy with the angels, to whom the Son of God promises we shall be made like by His grace!"—*Bossuet.*

3   The state of grace is sometimes called the "state of charity."—*Publisher, 2013.*

joy of which he had been deprived by sin, may be restored to him. Now this joy is nothing else than the wine of heavenly love, *which rejoices the heart of man.*

The same may not be said of works of charity as of sin; for the works of the just man are not effaced, abolished, or annihilated by supervening sin, but only forgotten; while the sin of the wicked man is not only forgotten, but effaced, abolished, and annihilated by holy penance. Wherefore, a just man's sin does not vivify forgiven sins, for they were entirely annihilated; but love, returning to the soul of the penitent, restores life to former good works, because they were not annihilated, but only cast into oblivion. It is not reasonable that sin should have as much power against charity, as charity against sin; for sin proceeds from our weakness, but charity from the divine omnipotence. If *sin abounds* in malice to destroy, *grace superabounds* to repair; and the *mercy* of God, by which sin is forgiven, is gloriously magnified above His *justice* by which the good works preceding sin are forgotten. Thus in all the corporal cures which Our Lord miraculously wrought, He not only restored health, but added such new benedictions as made the excellence of the cure surpass the virulence of the malady, so good is He towards men.[4]

---

4   "In the reconciliation of man with God, it is not man who makes the sacrifice. God was not the first to break friendship; on the contrary, He had loaded us with His favors. Man was the aggressor; what insolence! But God forgives and forgets. And if he who forgives once, and he who is forgiven, submit voluntarily to the laws of reconciled friendship, what ought to be the gratitude of him to whom many and grievous injuries are forgiven? It is an unquestionable truth, then, that the reconciled sinner owes to God a more earnest friendship than the just man who perseveres in his fidelity. This friendship, like a plant once dead, but resuscitated, casts deeper roots, lest it should be again destroyed. Hearts become like knots, more tightly joined; and as bones become firmer in places where they had been broken, on account of

When Nabuzardan destroyed Jerusalem, and Israel was led into captivity, the sacred fire of the altar was hidden in a well, where it was changed into mud; but this mud being drawn from the well, and placed in the sun at the time of the return from captivity, the dead fire resuscitated, and the mud was converted into flames. Thus, when the just man becomes the slave of sin, all the good works which he had performed are miserably forgotten, and reduced to mud; but on his departure from captivity, when by penance he returns to the grace of Divine Love, his preceding good works are drawn from the well of oblivion, and, touched by the rays of celestial mercy, revive, and are transformed into flames as bright as ever they had been, to be placed again on the sacred altar of the divine approbation, and to receive back their former dignity, merit, and value.

---

the extraordinary assistance brought by nature to the injured parts, so friends, who meet again in charity, display such affection to renew their broken friendship, that it remains ever after solid and inviolable."—*Bossuet.*

CHAPTER FOURTEEN

HOW FULL OF MERCY GOD IS, EVEN TOWARDS THE DAMNED

WE OUGHT to feel extreme pleasure in considering how God exercises His mercy by so many different favors to angels and to men, in Heaven and on earth, and how He exercises His justice in an endless variety of pains and chastisements; for His justice and His mercy are equally amiable and admirable in themselves, since both are nothing else than the one selfsame divinity. But inasmuch as the effects of His justice are full of bitterness, He sweetens them always with a mixture of His mercy, so that in the midst of the deluge of His just indignation, the green olive is preserved, and the devout soul, like a chaste dove, is able at length to find the verdant branch, if only it will lovingly ponder and meditate, after the manner of doves. Thus death, afflictions, labors, which, by the just ordinance of God, are the punishments of sin, are also, by His sweet mercy, so many ladders to ascend to Heaven, so many means to increase in grace, so many merits to obtain glory. Blessed then are poverty, hunger, sadness, sickness, death, persecution; for they are truly the just punishments of our sins, but punishments so tempered, and as doctors say, so perfumed, with the divine sweetness, kindness and clemency, that their bitterness is made agreeable. It is a strange thing, but true, that if the damned were not blinded by their obstinacy and hatred against God, they would find consolation in their pains, and behold the divine mercy admirably blended with the flames that burn them eternally. So true is this, that the saints considering, on the one hand, the terrible and horrible torments of the damned, praise the divine justice, crying out: Thou art just, O God! Thou art equitable; justice has ever reigned in Thy judgments. But considering, on the other, that these pains, though eternal and incomprehensible, are much less than the crimes for which they are inflicted, deserve; and filled with astonishment at the infinite mercy of God, they exclaim: O Lord, Thou art good, since even in the height of Thy wrath, Thou canst not contain the torrent of Thy mercies, but their waters flow out over the impetuous flames of Hell!

Chapter Fifteen

The Excellence of Abandonment to God

ABANDONMENT is the virtue of virtues; it is the cream of charity, the fragrance of humility, the sweetness of patience, and the fruit of perseverance. Great is this virtue, and worthy of being practiced by the beloved children of God.

"My Father," says our good Saviour on the cross, "into Thy hands I commend my spirit." (*Luke* 23:46). It is true He was pleased to say: "All is consummated," and "I have accomplished all that Thou gavest me to do," (*John* 19:30, and 17:4); but nevertheless, if it be Thy will that I remain still on the cross to suffer more, I am content; I resign my soul into Thy hands; do with it as pleases Thee.

Thus we should act on all occasions, whether in joy or sorrow; surrendering ourselves to the Divine Will, to be guided according to its good pleasure, without any concern about our own particular desires.[1]

Our Lord loves with an extremely tender love all those who abandon themselves entirely to His paternal care, allowing themselves to be governed by His Divine Providence, without considering whether its dealings towards them are sweet or bitter, being assured that everything coming from His paternal Heart will be for their good and advantage. Placing their confidence in God, they say: "My Father, I commend my soul, my body, all that I possess, into Thy hands, that Thou mayest do with them in Thy love what pleases Thee; whatever happens, nothing will move me from my firm resolution of acquiescing in the divine will concerning me and all that belongs to me; I wish to bury my will in that of God, or rather I wish Our Lord to will in me and for me, according to His good pleasure: I cast the care of myself into His hands."

Sometimes Our Lord wishes that souls chosen for the service of His Divine Majesty should nourish and fortify in themselves a resolution of following Him through all disgusts, aridities, repugnances, and bitternesses of a spiritual life, without consolation, tenderness, or enjoyment, and that they should believe themselves deserving of no other treatment; thus treading in the footsteps of our Divine Saviour, without any support but the Divine Will.

---

1   St. Teresa wrote to her director: "The state of my soul is, that I wish nothing but what God wishes. The will and good pleasure of God are so blended with my desires and inclinations that I have no other wish than His; it seems to me even that I could not have any other; I sigh for it alone, and in all things; I keep this disposition ever in my heart. I have no need of multiplying acts of submission to the will of God; I love all that God wills, and in His will I sovereignly rejoice."

Never shall we be reduced to such an extremity as to be unable to offer to the Divine Majesty a holy submission to the divine will.

We must possess a continual and imperturbable equanimity amid the great variety of human occurrences, and though all things change around us, remain immovable, with our eyes fixed on God alone. And though all things, I will not merely say around us, but even within us, should turn topsy-turvy; whether our souls be joyful or sorrowful, in peace or in trouble, in light or in darkness, in temptation or in repose, in happiness or in disgust; though the sun scorch, or the dew refresh; we should always keep our will fixed on the good pleasure of God, as its sole and supreme object.[2]

It is true that we require great confidence to abandon ourselves, without any reserve, to Divine Providence; but when we do abandon all, Our Lord takes care of all, and disposes of all. But if we reserve anything which we are unwilling to confide to Him, He leaves us, as if He would say: You think yourselves sufficiently wise to manage that affair without Me; you can do so, and see what will come of it.

St. Magdalen, who was wholly abandoned to Our Lord, remained at His feet, and listened while He spoke; and when He ceased to speak, she ceased to listen, but she did not move away from Him; thus her soul, abandoned to

---

2   A soul that lives on the dry bread of tribulation, that finds itself void of all good, that continually beholds its poverty, unworthiness, and corruption, that never ceases to seek God, though He seems to reject it, that seeks Him alone, not itself in God, is far above a soul that is anxious to know its perfection, that is disturbed at losing sight thereof, and that always wishes to receive some new caresses from God.

Our Lord, remained in His arms as a child in the bosom of its mother, which, when she puts it down to walk, walks until its mother takes it up again, and when she carries it, allows itself to be carried. It knows not, cares not, whither she goes; but is carried or led as its mother pleases; in like manner, the soul which loves the good pleasure of God in all that happens to it, either allows itself to be carried, or walks if necessary, doing at all times, with great care, the signified will of God.

CHAPTER SIXTEEN

CONFORMITY TO THE WILL OF GOD

L OOK not to the matter of your actions, which may
be contemptible in itself, but to the honor they possess in being willed by God, ordered in His Providence,
arranged in His wisdom. Purity of heart consists in valu-
ing all things according to the weights of the sanctuary,
which are nothing else than the will of God; do not love,
then, anything too ardently, not even virtue, which we
sometimes lose, by wishing for it beyond the bounds of
moderation.

Our center is the will of God; God wishes that I should
do this action now, God desires this matter of me, what
more is necessary? While I do this, I am not obliged to do
anything else.

O God! May Thy will be done, not only in the execution of Thy commandments, counsels, and inspirations,
which we ought to obey, but also in suffering the afflictions

which befall us; may Thy will be done in us and by us in everything that pleases Thee![1]

The truly loving heart loves the divine good pleasure, not only in consolations, but in afflictions; it even loves pains, crosses, and labors more, because the chief mark of love is, that it makes the lover suffer for the beloved. And why should we not endure the same hand of the Lord when it dispenses afflictions as when it distributes consolations? Oh, how good a thing it is to live only in God, to labor only in God, to rejoice only in God!

Oh, if the holy will of God reigned in us, how happy should we be! We should never commit any sin, or live according to our irregular inclinations, for that holy will is the rule of all excellence and sanctity. It is self-love, says St. Bernard, that burns eternally in Hell, for it ruins and destroys whatever it touches. If found in *Heaven*, it is cast out; for the angels were banished only because of self-will, because they wished to become like God, and on that account were precipitated into Hell. If found on *earth*, it robs man of grace, and subjects him to death, as [happened] to our first parents in the terrestrial paradise. In a word, it brings misfortune alone; and, therefore, when we discover anything within us not conformed to the will of God, we should prostrate ourselves before Him, and say to Him that we detest and disown our own will, and everything in us

---

1   A soul truly submissive to the will of God is attached to nothing created; it knows that all things, out of God, are vanity and nothingness; hence it has no other end or object in view than to die to itself, and to be resigned fully, always, and in all things.—*Bl. Henry Suso.*

    St. Vincent de Paul excelled in this point, living detached from himself and from all creatures. His constant endeavor was to be conformed to the good pleasure of God, and to adore lovingly the arrangements of His Providence.

that could displease Him, or that is contrary to His holy love, promising Him never to wish for anything but what will be conformable to His divine good pleasure.

Let us open the arms of our will, embrace lovingly the cross, and acquiesce in the most holy will of God, singing to Him this hymn of resignation and conformity: "Thy will be done on earth as it is in Heaven."

Chapter Seventeen

Practice of Conformity to the Will of God

CAST your eyes over the general will of God, by which He wills all the works of His mercy and justice that are in Heaven, on earth, and under the earth; and, with a profound humility, approve, praise, and love this holy, just, amiable, and supreme will. Cast your eyes, next, over the special will of God, by which He loves His friends, and bestows on them various gifts of consolation and tribulation; dwell some time on this thought, considering the diversity of consolations, but particularly the tribulations, which the good endure; then, with a great humility, approve, praise, and love this will.

Consider this will in regard to yourself, in everything good or ill that happens, or can happen, to you, except sin; then approve, praise, and love it, protesting that you wish ever to honor, cherish, and adore this sovereign will, committing to it your person and all that belongs to you. Finally, conclude, with great confidence in this holy will, that it will do everything necessary for your good and happiness.

Oh, what a consolation for us, if we were accustomed to receive all things from the paternal hand of Him who, in opening it, fills every living creature with His blessing! What unction would sweeten our pains! What honey and oil should we draw from the hardest rocks! What moderation should accompany us in prosperity, since God would only send us adversity to draw from it His own glory and our salvation. Let us think well on this truth, and regard only God in all events, and all events only in God.

We must know that the abandonment of our will means properly the surrender of it to God; for it will avail us nothing to renounce ourselves, unless we become united to the Divine Goodness.

But we sometimes see persons, who, coming to the service of God, say: Lord! I commend my spirit into Thy hands, but on condition that Thou wilt always give me consolations, without anything to contradict my will, and wilt give me superiors in all respects according to my liking.

Alas! What are you doing? Do you not see that this is not to resign your soul into the hands of God, as Our Lord did? Do you not know that this is only one of those reserves from which all our troubles, disquietudes, and other imperfections, usually arise? For, as soon as things happen not according to our expectations and anticipations, a sudden desolation seizes on our poor souls. Why is this, unless because we are not resigned with indifference into the hands of God? Oh, how happy should we be, if we faithfully practiced this virtue! Undoubtedly, we should arrive at the highest perfection of a St. Catherine of Siena, of a St. Francis, of a St. Angela of Foligno, and of many others. Consider that the eternal Son of God came Himself to teach us this submission and reverence due to the supreme will, not only by informing us in words that He had not come to do His own will, but that of His Father, but still more by the example of His resignation: "My Father! If it be possible, let this chalice pass away from me; yet not my will, but Thine be done." And our divine Master taught us to ask every day that the will of God should be done on earth as it is in Heaven; and, in fine, He concluded the course of His mortal life by the surrender of Himself to the will and disposal of His Eternal Father: "My Father! Into Thy hands I commend my spirit."

Act then thus, and say with Our Lord on all occasions: *My God, I commend my spirit*, absolutely and unreservedly, *Into Thy hands;* dost Thou wish me to be in aridity or in consolation? To be contradicted? To meet with difficulties and repugnances? To be loved or not loved? In all events, *I commend my spirit into Thy hands*. Let those, therefore, who are employed in the exercises of an active life not desire to exchange them for those of a contemplative, and let those who contemplate not quit their contemplation until God commands it; let us be silent when necessary, and speak when necessary. If we act in this manner, we shall be able to say, at the hour of death, in imitation of our Divine Saviour: *It is consummated;* my God! All is consummated; I have accomplished Thy divine will in the various occurrences that happened to me by Thy Providence; what remains for me now to do, but to commend my spirit into Thy hands at the decline of my life, as I gave it to Thee at the beginning of it, and during its course?

O my God! Conduct me by Thy will; grant me to pass through cold, heat, light, darkness, labor, repose; though Thou shouldst lead me to the gates of death, I shall fear nothing in Thy company.

O heavenly Father! May Thy will be done on earth, where consolations are rare, and labors innumerable. And thou, O my soul! Take it as thy daily practice to say, when anything painful befalls thee: Not my will, but that of my God be done!

CHAPTER EIGHTEEN

GOD IS OUR FATHER[1]

T O BLESS and thank God for all the appointments of His Providence is indeed a holy occupation; but if, while abandoning ourselves to God that He may do whatever He wishes with us, without attending on our part to what happens—though we are not expected to be quite devoid of feeling—we could divert our minds to the Divine Goodness: praising it not in the effects which it ordains, but in itself, and in its own excellence, then, without doubt, we should perform an exercise much more holy. Let us employ a parable, since this method was most agreeable to the sovereign Master of that love which we teach.

---

1   "What district of Palestine did not experience, a thousand and a thousand times, His kindness? I doubt not but He would have sought the miserable to the ends of the earth, if His Father's order had not detained Him in Judea. Did He ever see a miserable sufferer, without being moved to pity? Ah! How enrapturing it is to find in the Gospel, that He never undertakes any important cure, but first of all He manifests some tokens of compassion! There are a thousand beautiful instances of this in the Gospel. The first favor He grants is to sympathize for the afflicted with a truly paternal affection; His heart hears the voice of misery which invokes it, and His arm is moved to bestow relief."—*Bossuet.*

The daughter of an excellent surgeon and physician suffered from a long continued fever, and knowing that her father loved her exceedingly, she said one day to a friend of hers: "I feel much pain, but still I never think of remedies; for I know not what would cure me. I might desire one thing, and another thing might be necessary for me. Do I not gain more by leaving this care to my father, who knows, wishes, and is able to procure everything conducive to my health? It would be painful for me to think, but he thinks sufficiently for me; it would be painful for me to wish for anything, but he wishes for everything serviceable to me. I have only to await what he judges expedient, and when he is near, employ myself only in testifying to him my filial love and perfect confidence." And after these words she slept, while her father, judging it proper that she should be bled, arranged what was requisite, and coming to her as soon as she awoke, after having inquired how the sleep had benefited her, asked if she would not like to be bled in order to be cured. "My father," she answered, "I am yours, I do not know what I ought to wish for, to cure me; it is for you to wish and to do for me whatever appears to you good; as for me, it is enough for me to honor and to love you with all my heart, as I always do." Her arm was then bandaged, and her father held the lance over the vein; but neither while he pierced the flesh, nor while the blood sprang forth, did this amiable daughter cast her eyes once on the wounded arm, or the gushing blood, but, with looks fixed on her father's countenance, she only said, now and again, softly and sweetly: "My father loves me well, and I am all his." And when everything was over, she did not thank him, but only repeated once more the selfsame words of her affection and filial confidence.

Tell me, now; did not this young girl testify a more tender and sincere love towards her father, than if she had employed a great deal of time in inquiries about the remedies for her disease, in gazing on the scarlet stream, or in uttering words of gratitude? No doubt, whatever, about it. For, by thinking of herself, what would she have gained unless anxiety, since her father thought sufficiently for her? By looking on her arm, what would have resulted, unless, perhaps, to get a fright? And by thanking her father, what virtue would she have practiced, but gratitude? Did she not then act better by confining her attention to some demonstrations of filial love, infinitely more agreeable to a father than any other virtue?

My eyes are always on the Lord, for He will free my feet from pits and snares. Have you fallen into the snares of trials? Regard not your misfortune; look only to God; He will have care of you. *Cast thy solicitude on Him, and He will provide for thee.* Why trouble yourself by sighing or pining about the accidents of this world, since you know not what you ought to wish for, and God will always wish what is best for you? Await, then, in repose of spirit, the effects of the divine good pleasure, and let it suffice for you, since it is always good; so Our Lord ordered St. Catherine of Siena, saying: "Think of Me, and I will think of thee."[2]

---

2 God takes extraordinary care of your life. You were yet an infant, borne in the bosom of your mother, and without distrust of her, affectionate as she was, He carried you in His arms. He aided you to form your first steps, and has always led you by the hand. If He permitted you to fall, it was to teach you your own weakness; the fall has not been fatal; you fell under His hand, and He has raised you up.

If you are tempted, He assists you; if shaken, He steadies you; if in sin, He

Look then, a hundred times a day, on the loving will of God; and placing our will in the divine will, let us exclaim devoutly: O infinitely sweet goodness! How amiable is Thy will! How desirable are Thy favors! Thou hast created us for eternal life, and thy maternal breast, enlarged with the sacred paps of incomparable love, abounds in the milk of mercy, whether to forgive the penitent, or to perfect the just. Why then, should we not cast our wills into Thine, as little children nestle in the bosom of their mother, to drink in the milk of Thy eternal benedictions?

---

endures you; if penitent, He forgives you. You retire to rest; He watches over you. Are you sick? He is around your bed, on the right hand and on the left, to comfort you, whichever way you turn. There Ezechias found Him, prayed to Him, and was heard. For you He tempers the heats of the day, and the evil influences of the night. Never did father so much love his children as God loves you. Your defects disfigure you in the eyes of men, who often cannot endure you; but our heavenly Father finds His children amiable. He loves all His works; but He singularly loves man, made to His image.

Chapter Nineteen

We Should Serve God Our Father for Love

THE SON serves as a son, and not as a slave, through fear of punishment, nor as a mercenary, through hope of recompense, but only in order to please his father, and give evidence of that love which is so deeply imprinted in the filial heart. Whence it comes that when the soul has conceived a fear of losing paradise, it passes further and exclaims: Though there were no paradise, God is my Father; He has created me, preserves me, nourishes me, gives me everything; and therefore I wish to love, honor, and serve Him perfectly.

O gift of piety, rich present which God bestows on the heart! Blessed is he who has the dispositions of a filial heart towards the paternal heart of our heavenly Father. These are the dispositions He would have us learn from the Lord's Prayer, desiring us to address Him as Our

Father Who art in Heaven: a name of respect, of love, and of fear.[1]

To show you that this gift of piety, that is to say, a filial fear, is given us by the Holy Ghost, the Apostle St. Paul, writing to the Romans, says: "We have not received the spirit of fear and bondage, but the spirit of adoption of children of God, whereby we call Him Father"; as if he should say: we have become like little children near Our Lord. Little children live in great confidence; they never think that their father either wishes to beat them, or is preparing an inheritance for them; but only think of loving him, because they are carried in his arms, and are cherished and provided for in every way by the care of their good father. Thus ought we to act towards God, honoring Him as our most amiable Father, serving Him with love, without apprehending chastisement, or claiming remuneration, allowing ourselves to be carried in the arms of His holy Providence whithersoever He pleases.

---

1   "We owe a filial affection to God. This, the sweetest and most excellent of domestic sentiments, God claims as a Father. We are really His children. Does not St. Paul say: By the grace of regeneration and Baptism we have become the children of God, and received the grace of the divine adoption?"—*Père de Ravignan.*

CHAPTER TWENTY

HOW JEALOUS GOD IS OF OUR HEART

THIS jealousy is not a jealousy of covetousness, but a jealousy of the highest friendship; for it is not His interest that we love Him, it is our own. Our love is useless to Him, but profitable to us; and if agreeable to Him, is only so because profitable to us; for, being the sovereign good, He is pleased to communicate Himself through love, without the possibility of receiving any good in return. Hence He cries out, complaining of sinners, in a kind of jealousy: "They have left Me, the fountain of living water, and have dug to themselves cisterns, broken cisterns that can hold no water." See, I beg of you, how delicately our divine Spouse expresses the nobility and generosity of His jealousy. "They have left Me," He says, "the fountain of living water;" as if He would say: I do not complain of their leaving Me, on account of any injury that I can sustain thereby; for what injury can a fountain sustain, if no one draws water from it? Does it cease to flow over the land, because abandoned? But I regret their misfortune, for, having *left Me,* they are pleased with *wells without any water.* And if, by any possibility, they could find another fountain of living water, I might easily endure their departure from Me, since I have no other wish for their love than the desire of their happiness. It is, therefore, for our own sakes He wishes we should love Him; because we cannot cease to love Him without entering on the path of our destruction, and because whatever affections we deprive Him of, we only waste.

Chapter Twenty-One

An Admirable Model of Perfect Abandonment

W E MAY believe that the most holy Virgin Our Blessed Lady derived so much contentment from carrying her dear little Jesus in her arms, that this contentment prevented weariness, or at least made it agreeable; for, if to carry a twig of "agnus-castus" refreshes travelers, what alleviation would not the glorious Mother receive from carrying the immaculate Lamb of God? And if, sometimes, she allowed Him to walk beside her, holding Him by the hand, it was not that she would not much prefer to have Him on her bosom, with His arms round her neck, but it was because she wished to exercise Him in forming His steps, and to support Himself. And we, like our heavenly Father's little children, can also advance in two ways: first, by the steps of our own will, when we conform it to His, holding the hand of His divine will by that of our obedience, and following wherever He conducts us, that is to say, doing what He signifies to be His wish—for when He wishes anything to be done, He always gives the power to do it; and secondly, we can accompany Our Lord, without any trouble of our own, merely allowing ourselves to be carried by Him, according to the divine good pleasure, as an infant in the arms of its mother, by an admirable agreement, which is called the union, or rather the unity, of our will with that of God.

If anyone had asked the sweet Infant Jesus in the arms of His Mother whither He went, might He not reasonably have replied: I go nowhere; it is my Mother who goes for me? And if He had been questioned: But, at least, do you not go with your Mother? Might He not reasonably have answered: No: I go nowhere, or if I go where my Mother carries me, it is not by my own steps I go, but by the steps of my Mother? And if the inquiry had been continued: but at least, O dear divine Infant, you wish to allow yourself to be carried by your blessed Mother? "No, certainly," He might have said, "I wish for nothing of the kind;" but as my good Mother travels for me, so she wishes for me; I leave to her the care of going and coming for me, as appears to her good; and as I only walk by her steps, so I only wish by her desires. When I find myself in her arms, I pay no attention to this or that, but leave every care to my Mother, except the one of resting on her bosom, of nourishing myself with her virginal milk, and of holding fast to her most amiable neck, while I lovingly kiss her *with the kisses of My mouth.* And while I enjoy the delights of these holy caresses, which surpass all expression, it seems to me that my Mother is a tree of life, and that I am her fruit, or that I am her very heart in the midst of her bosom, or her soul in the midst of her heart; therefore, as her steps suffice for her and me, without my making one, so her will suffices for her and me, without my taking any concern about her going or coming; neither am I troubled, whether she goes quickly or slowly, or from one side to the other; nor do I inquire to what place she goes; being content that, whatever happens, I am in her arms, and on her virginal bosom, where *I feast Myself among the lilies.* O Divine Child of Mary! Grant to my poor soul some of these transports of holy love. Go then, most amiable dear little Child! Or rather go not, but remain resting on the bosom of Thy sweet Mother; go always with her and by her, and never go without her, so long as Thou art a child. *Blessed is the womb that bore Thee, and the paps that gave Thee suck!*

This is the manner in which we ought, like wax, to be pliable in the hands of the divine good pleasure, not wasting our time in fretting about events, but allowing God to do for us as pleases Him, according to the words of the great Apostle: "Cast your solicitude on Him, for He has care of you." He says: "All your solicitude," that is, both present and future; for He will have care of the success of our undertakings, and of wishing for us whatever is best.

CHAPTER TWENTY-TWO

IT IS GOOD TO ABANDON ONESELF TO PROVIDENCE

THE Providence of God is infinite and admirable; it reaches to all things, reigns over all things, and turns all things to its glory. He who considers well the doings of Providence, the daily and universal commerce which creatures carry on, with such extraordinary harmony, for the service of man, must be moved with a thousand loving emotions towards the supreme wisdom, and cry out: Thy Providence, O Eternal Father, governs us most wonderfully!

First, God furnishes men with all means necessary to attain their end. The visible sun communicates his light and heat to the universe; without him, there would be neither worth nor beauty in the world; he is the universal principle of life to inferior things, giving them the vigor they require. In like manner, the Divine Goodness animates all souls to gain their salvation, and encourages all hearts to its love and service, without anyone being able to hide from its celestial influences. With this intention God made us to His own image and likeness at creation, and made Himself to our image and likeness at the Incarnation, after which He suffered death, to redeem the whole human race and reinstate it in life.

We ought, indeed, a hundred times a day, to cast our eyes on the loving Providence of God, who has His Heart always turned towards us by foresight, as we should have ours always turned towards Him by confidence; and, placing our hearts in His divine will, we should cry out devoutly: O infinitely sweet goodness! How amiable is Thy will! How desirable are Thy favors! Thou hast created us for eternal life, and Thy maternal breast, enlarged with the sacred paps of incomparable love, abounds in the milk of mercy, whether to forgive the penitent, or to perfect the just. Why, then, do we not hang our wills on Thine, as little children nestle themselves in the bosom of their mothers, to drink the milk of Thy eternal benedictions? Oh! How true it is that God is a thousand and a thousand times more worthy of being loved than He is loved![1]

My God! What pleasure should our understanding take in the frequent thought of Thy divinity, since it is so good, so sweet, so beautiful, so kind towards all, so willing to communicate itself! Would it not be happy to love of

---

1   *"Be not solicitous,* or uneasy, says the Saviour; consider how the raven, one of the most voracious birds, nevertheless, without barns or provisions, without sowing or labor-ing, finds its nourishment. God supplies what is needful for it and *its little ones who invoke Him,* says the Psalmist. God hears their cries, though harsh and discordant, and nourishes them as well as the nightingales and others whose voices are sweeter and more harmonious."—*Bossuet.*

necessity this infinite beauty and incomprehensible Goodness, as is done by the blessed spirits, who are constrained by a most sweet and inevitable necessity to love it eternally?

Ah, how much God loves us! How sweetly He protects and guides us! He wishes us to be entirely His; let us not seek, then, other arms to rest in than those of His Providence; let us not cast our looks elsewhere; let us repose our mind on Him alone; let us keep our will united to His, that His and ours may be only one; let us wish sweetly whatever He wishes; let us allow Him to govern us; let us not reflect so much upon ourselves; let us forever live on the mercy of His Providence; all will go well when our soul has no other retreat than in God, and the train of our affairs will succeed more prosperously when He assists us. Can the child perish who is in the arms of an Almighty Father?

Desire nothing; resign your cares to Divine Providence; allow God to do with you whatever He pleases, as little children surrender themselves to their nurses. Let Him carry you on His right arm, or on His left, as He chooses; an infant does not take offence at either; if He would lay you down, or lift you up, permit Him, for, like a good nurse, He knows better than ourselves what we need. I mean to say that if Divine Providence permits trials or afflictions to befall you, refuse them not, but accept them willingly, tranquilly, and lovingly; if He permits them not, desire them not; and thus you will keep your heart always prepared for the divine dispensations.

Everyone knows how to be resigned amid the joys and happiness of prosperity, but to be so amid storms and tempests is peculiar to the children of God. Let the heavens combine against me, let the earth and the elements rebel, let every creature declare war against my existence, I fear not; it is enough for me that God is with me, and I with Him.

Let Our Lord turn and push us to the right or to the left; let Him, as with new Jacobs, hold us fast, and give us a hundred turns; let Him force us sometimes on one side, sometimes on the other; in a word, let Him deal us a thousand injuries; yet we will not let Him go, until He gives us His eternal benediction. Thus our good God will never abandon us, unless to hold us better; He will never leave us, unless to guard us better; He will never wrestle with us, unless to yield to us and bless us.

O God! What a happiness to be thus resigned to the good pleasure of our sweet Saviour, by an abandonment of our whole being to His holy Providence! How happy should we be, if, submitting our will to that of God, we would adore it equally in times of tribulation and of consolation, assured that all events proceed from His divine hand for our advantage, to purify and refine us in holy charity!

Let us, therefore, embark on the sea of Divine Providence, without biscuit, without oars, without sails, in a word, without any supplies; let us leave the care of our affairs to Our Lord, without any fear; His goodness will provide sufficiently for all.[2]

---

2   The following beautiful lines were written by St. Francis de Sales to a nun: "Yesterday, I crossed the lake in a little boat, to visit the Archbishop of Vienne. I was very much at home to have no other support than a thin plank, as I could rest more securely on holy Providence; and I was still more comfortable in being under obedience there to the ferryman, who ordered us all to be seated, and to keep steady, without stirring, as seemed good to him to be done, and, indeed, I did not move. But, my daughter, do not take these words as of any great value: no, they are only little imaginations of virtues that my heart makes to recreate itself; when there is real danger, I am not so brave."

Our Lord has taught me from my youth to confide in Providence, and if I were to be born again I would desire to be governed, even in the least things, by His holy Providence, with the simplicity of a child, and with a profound contempt for all human prudence. It is a great enjoyment to me to walk with eyes closed, under the guidance of Providence, whose designs are impenetrable, but are always sweet and amiable to those who confide in them. Let us leave our soul, then, in the barque of Providence; it will conduct us safely to port. Happy are they who confide in Him who as God is able, as a Father is willing, to grant us everything good; miserable, on the contrary, are they who trust in creatures; which promise great things, give little, and make the purchaser pay dearly for the little they give.

Since the Providence of God is such as we have described it, let us belong in such a manner to God, that we may belong to no one else; for no one can serve two masters.

Should we not be content to leave our life, and all that we possess, to the pure disposal of this adorable Providence? For we are no longer our own, but the property of Him who, to make us His, was pleased, in so loving a manner, to become entirely ours.

Providence defers its assistance only to excite our confidence. If our heavenly Father does not always grant what we ask, it is to keep us near Him, and to give us occasion of pressing Him by a loving violence, as He showed well to the two pilgrims of Emmaus, with whom He would not have tarried, only that, as the day was drawing to a close, they prevailed on Him.

Let nothing separate us from His holy love; let our heart, whether languishing, or dying, or living, have never any life but in Him, and for Him, and let Him be forever the God of our heart.

Let the storm and the tempest come; you shall not perish; you are with Jesus. If fear seize on you, cry out: O Saviour, save me! He will reach out His hand; grasp it, and proceed joyfully, without philosophizing on your mishap. So long as St. Peter had confidence, the tempest could not harm him; when he feared, he sank. Fear is often a greater danger than the danger itself.

As for me, there are times when it appears to me that I have not strength to resist, and that if an occasion presented itself, I should succumb; but I only place my confidence the more in God, and hold as certain, that in presence of the occasion God will support me with His strength, and that I shall destroy my enemies as so many little lambkins.

When you feel that, on account of the multitude of your imperfections, confidence is wanting to you to have recourse to Our Lord, let the superior part of your soul rejoice, using some words of hope and love to Our Lord, with more earnestness and more frequency than usual.

Be very careful not to become disturbed after having fallen into any fault, nor to yield to compassionate emotions over yourself, which proceed from pride; but humble yourself promptly before God, with a sweet and loving humility, that will lead you to have recourse confidently and immediately to His goodness, being assured of His assistance to you to amend.

When you fall, prostrate yourself before God to say to Him in a spirit of confidence and humility: Mercy! O Lord, for I am weak! Raise us up again in peace, and join again the thread of Thy love, to continue Thy work. We have imperfections; but it is necessary to be content with being men and not angels, to despise temptations, to go forward without regard to them, and to banish diffidence by the thought that God is more merciful than we are miserable. Suffer, undisturbed, the want of sensible[3] consolation, a single act of virtue made in time of aridity being of much more value than many made with a stronger, though less agreeable love. In fine, make a peaceful abandonment of yourself to Providence in the various occurrences of life, and even in the presence of death. God has watched over you until the present; hold fast by the hand of His Providence, and He will assist you; and, where you cannot walk, He will carry you.

I hope that God will strengthen you more and more; and, at the thought, or rather temptation, that your present fervor will not continue, answer once for all that those who confide in God shall never be confounded, and that as you have cast, both for soul and body, your care on the Lord, He will not fail to provide for you. Let us serve God well today; He will take care of tomorrow. Every day should carry its own burden. Have no anxiety about tomorrow; for God who reigns today will reign tomorrow. Either He will not send you adversity, or if He will send it, He will give you an invincible courage to meet it. If assaulted by

---

3   Sensible—of the senses, of the feelings.—*Publisher,* 2013.

temptations, desire not to be freed from them. It is good that we should experience them, in order to have an opportunity of combating them, and of gaining victories. This serves as an exercise in the most excellent virtues, thus grounded deeply in the soul.

Moreover, keep your eyes lifted up to God; erect your courage on holy humility, strengthen it in meekness, confirm it in equanimity; let your mind be ever master of its inclinations; and allow no apprehensions to seize upon your heart. You have already passed through many dangers, and it was by the grace of God you did so; the same grace will be near you on all succeeding occasions, and will deliver you from difficulties, one after another, though an angel from Heaven should be required to guide your wavering steps.

Cast not your eyes on your infirmities and insufficiencies, unless to become more humble: never to be discouraged. Often look on your right hand to God and the two angels whom He has appointed to you: one for your own person, another for the direction of your little family. Say to these holy angels: Sirs, how shall we act? Beseech them to furnish you with a knowledge of the divine will, and to contemplate the inspirations which Our Lady would wish you to receive from her paps of love. Regard not the variety of imperfections that live in you, and in all those persons whom Our Lord and Our Lady have confided to you, unless to increase in a holy fear of offending God, but never to be surprised; for it is not a wonderful thing that each herb and flower in a garden should require a particular kind of care.

Chapter Twenty-Three

Fear and Hope

TO WALK securely in this life, we must always walk between fear and hope: between fear of the judgments of God, *which are unfathomable abysses,* and hope of His mercies, which are without number or measure, *and over all His works.*

We must fear the divine judgments, but without discouragement, and be encouraged at the sight of the mercies of God, without presumption.

Those who entertain an extreme and inordinate dread of being damned, show that they have more need of humility and submission than of understanding. We must indeed abase, annihilate, and lose our soul, but only to exalt, preserve, and save it. That humility which is prejudicial to charity is undoubtedly a false humility.

Whatever leads to discouragement, to despair, to trouble, is contrary to charity, which teaches us to make every effort, though *with fear and trembling,* but never to distrust the goodness of God, who wills all men to be saved, and to come to penance.

We serve a Master who is rich in mercy to those who invoke Him; He cancels a debt of ten thousand talents on a very brief petition. We must have sentiments worthy of His goodness, yet serve Him with fear; but while we tremble, we must not cease to rejoice: that humility which discourages is not a good humility.

CHAPTER TWENTY-FOUR

A WILL PERFECTLY RESIGNED

IMAGINE you behold the glorious and ever-admirable St. Louis setting sail for a foreign land, and the Queen, his wife, embarking with His Majesty. Suppose that someone inquires of this heroic princess: Where are you going, madam? She would undoubtedly answer: I am going wherever the King is going. But do you know where the King is going? She would say: He has told me in general; yet I have no anxiety to know where he is going, but only to go with him. Then, madam, you have no special purpose in this voyage? No, she would reply: I have no other than that of being with my dear lord and husband. The other might add: See, he goes to Egypt, to pass to Palestine; he will stay at Damascus, at Acre, and at many other places; do you not intend, madam, to reside there also? No, indeed, she would say; I have no intention unless to be near my King, and the places he will visit are of no consideration to me, unless inasmuch as he will be there; I shall go, without desiring to go, for I care about nothing but the presence of the King; it is the King who desires the voyage, and as for me, I desire no voyage, but only the presence of the King; journeys, delays, and everything else being quite indifferent to me. Thus, a will resigned to that of its God should have no other desire than simply to follow the will of God.

As he who sails on board a ship does not advance by his own motion, but by the motion of the vessel, so the heart embarked on board the divine good pleasure should have no other wish than that of being carried by the will of God. Then, no more will the heart be heard to say: Thy will be done, not mine; for it will no longer have any will to renounce; but it will say these words: Lord! Into Thy hands I commend my will; as if its will were no more at its own disposal, but only at that of the Divine Providence.

Among all the pleasures of perfect love, that which is found in the acquiescence of the soul to spiritual tribulations is unquestionably the purest and most refined. The Blessed Angela of Foligno gives us an admirable description of the interior pains which she sometimes endured: she says that her soul was in torment, like a man with his hands and feet tied, hanging by the neck between life and death, yet not strangled; without any hope of succor; unable to support himself with his feet, to assist himself with his hands, to cry out with his mouth, or even to sigh. It is really so; the soul is sometimes so pressed with interior afflictions, that all its powers and faculties are crushed and desolated by the absence of everything that could solace it, as well as by the dread and apprehension of everything that could sadden it. To such an extent that, after the example of its Saviour, it begins to grow weary, to fear, to shudder, then to be sad with a sadness like that of the dying, when it can well exclaim: "My soul is sorrowful even unto death;" and, with the consent of its whole interior, it desires, implores, and beseeches that, "If it be possible, this chalice may pass away from it," remaining attached only by the finest point of the spirit to the heart and good pleasure of God, and making one simple act of acquiescence: "O Eternal Father, may my will be never done, but Thine!" And it is remarkable that the soul makes this act of resignation in the midst of so much trouble, so many repugnances and contradictions, that it does not perceive itself doing so; at least it imagines that its acts are all so languid that they cannot come from the heart or be of any value, because what is regarded then as the divine good pleasure is endured not only without pleasure or contentment, but even contrary to the pleasure and contentment of the heart, which love allows to utter all the lamentations of Job and Jeremias, but on condition that one act of acquiescence should be made in the inmost depths, in the purest part of the soul. And this acquiescence is not sweet, or tender, or sensible, though it is real, and strong, and loving; it seems to have retired into the furthest corner of the soul, or, as it were, into the citadel of the fortress, where it remains courageous, though all the rest has fallen, and is overwhelmed with sadness. And the more removed this love is from aid, abandoned by the faculties of the soul, the more sublime is its constancy, and the nobler its fidelity.

CHAPTER TWENTY-FIVE

THE LOVE OF SUBMISSION, BY WHICH OUR WILL IS UNITED TO THE GOOD PLEASURE OF GOD

W E DO not conform ourselves to the divine will of good pleasure in the same manner as to the signified will of God, for the will of good pleasure has no need of our obedience in order to be accomplished: without us, and in spite of us, it will always be done. Nevertheless, we can honor it, and unite ourselves to it, by submitting to what it ordains: when love induces us to submit to it, we call it the love of submission.

But this union and conformity with the divine good pleasure is made, either by a holy resignation, or by a most holy indifference.

Resignation is practiced by way of effort: we would rather live than die; nevertheless, since it is the will of God that we should die, we are content. We would like to live if it were pleasing to God; and, moreover, we would like it to please God to let us live. We die willingly, but we would live much more willingly; we pass away satisfied, but we would remain much better satisfied. Job, in his sorrows, displayed this resignation. "If we have received good things," he says, "from the Lord, why should we not also receive evil things?" He speaks of supporting and enduring trials. "As it hath pleased the Lord, so is it done; blessed be the name of the Lord." These are words of acceptance and resignation, uttered by way of patience and endurance.

This resignation is agreeable to God, for the love which produces it is great; but it attains its highest excellence when we *cherish, love,* and *embrace* sufferings, on account of the divine good pleasure which sends them to us.[1]

---

1   "I am acquainted with your state, and my soul, far from being afflicted, is dilated with joy. Never was my heart so much united to yours before. Remain, then, a victim to Providence, by an entire abandonment, since God has chosen you for the object of His delights. What He wishes to do with you is good, and He will draw His glory from all. God makes use of what men call imprudence to conduct us to His ends, and to prove the purity of our love. He who abandons himself unreservedly to God on the most trying occasions, gives the highest testimony that a creature can give of a sincere love. To act in this manner is to become, in Jesus Christ, the beloved Son of God. Far from compassionating, I envy you. Peace of heart and resignation change torments into delights."—*Spiritual Letters.*

OF ST. FRANCIS DE SALES TO THE PIOUS READER

IT IS with all my heart, I say the word, "Adieu." To God (*A Dieu*) may you ever belong in this life, serving Him faithfully in the midst of the pains we all have in carrying our crosses, and in the immortal life, blessing Him eternally with all the celestial court. The greater good of our souls is to be with God; and the greatest good, to be with God alone.

He who is with God alone, is never sad, unless for having offended God, and his sadness then consists in a profound but tranquil and peaceful humility and submission, after which he rises again in the Divine Goodness, by a sweet and perfect confidence, without chagrin or vexation.

He who is with God alone seeks only God, and because God is no less in tribulation than in prosperity, he remains in peace during times of adversity.

He who is with God alone thinks often of Him in the midst of the occupations of this life.

He who is with God alone would be glad that everyone should know he wishes to serve God, and to be engaged in exercises suitable to keep him united to God.

Live then entirely to God; desire only to please Him, and to please creatures only in Him, and for Him. What greater blessing can I wish you? Thus, then, by this continual wish I make for your soul, I say: Adieu.

To God let us belong, without end, without reserve, without measure, as He is ours forever. May we always unite our little crosses with His great one!

To God let us live, and to God without anything more, since out of Him, and without Him, we seek for nothing: no, not even for ourselves, who, indeed, out of Him, and without Him, are only true nothings.

Adieu. I desire for you the abundance of Divine Love, which is and will be forever the only good of our hearts, given to us only for Him, who has given His Heart entirely to us.

Let Jesus be our crown! Let Mary be our hope! I am, in the name of the Son and the Mother,

Sincerely yours,

FRANCIS DE SALES

1. WE SHOULD NOT DESPAIR OF THE SALVATION OF ANY SINNER[1]

ST. FRANCIS de Sales, says the Bishop of Belley, never wished that the repentance of any sinner should be despaired of before his last breath, observing that this life was the way of our pilgrimage, in which those who walked might fall, and those who fell might, by grace, rise again, and, like the giants in the fable, they sometimes rose stronger than they had fallen, grace superabounding where sin had abounded.

He went still further; for, even after death, he did not wish that anyone should pass a bad judgment on those who had led a bad life, unless it regarded those of whose damnation we are assured by the truth of the Holy Scripture. Beyond this point, He would not allow anyone to seek to penetrate into the secrets of God, which are reserved to His wisdom.

---

1   We take this chapter from the *Spirit of St. Francis de Sales,* by Camus [Bishop of Belley].

His principal reason was, that, as the first grace of justification does not fall under the merit of any preceding work, so the last grace, which is that of final perseverance, is not given to any merit either. Besides, who has known the mind of the Lord, and who has been His counselor? For this reason, He wished that, even after the last breath, we should hope well of the deceased person, however sad an end he might have seemed to make, because we can only form very uncertain conjectures, founded on external appearances, in which the most experienced are often deceived.[2]

2. Sentiments of St. Francis de Sales on the Number of the Elect

The extreme gentleness of St. Francis de Sales, says the Bishop of Belley, from whom we borrow this chapter, always led him to the mildest opinions, however little probability they carried. We were conversing one day, in company, on this dreadful word of the Gospel: "Many are called, but few are chosen." Someone remarked that the number of the elect was called a little flock, as that of fools, or of the reprobate, was called infinite, and such things. He answered that he thought very few Christians (he spoke of those in the true Church, out of which there is no salvation) would be damned; because, he said, having the root of the True Faith, sooner or later it usually yields its fruit,

---

2 We read the following passage in the *Life of Père De Ravignan:* "In certain deaths there are hidden mysteries of mercy and strokes of grace, in which the eye of man beholds only the strokes of justice. By the gleams of the last light, God reveals Himself to souls whose greatest misfortune was to have been ignorant of Him; and the last sigh, understood by Him who searches hearts, may be a groan that asks for pardon."

which is salvation, and from being dead, becomes living by charity.

And when asked what, then, was the meaning of this word of the Gospel concerning the small number of the elect, he said that in comparison with the rest of the world and with infidel nations, the number of Christians was very small, but that of this small number there would be very few lost, according to this remarkable sentence: "There is no damnation for those who are in Jesus Christ." (*Rom.* 8:1). Which, indeed, is to be understood of justifying grace;[3] but this grace is not separated from a faith living and animated by charity. Moreover, as He who gives the grace to begin, gives also the grace to perfect the undertaking, so it is credible that the vocation to Christianity, which is a work of God, is a perfect work, and conducts to the end of all consummation, which is glory.

I added another reason, and he was pleased with it: that the mercy of God being above all His works, and swimming over His justice, as oil over vinegar, there was every reason for trusting in His own natural disposition to pity and forgive, abundantly shown forth in the copious redemption of the Saviour; and there was no sign for believing that God would have commenced to erect the salvation of the true Christian by faith, which is its foundation, without proceeding with it to the end, which consists in charity.

This doctrine is of great consolation, provided it does not make us negligent in doing good; for, it is not enough to say with the ancients: *The temple of the Lord, the temple*

---

3   Justifying grace—that is, Sanctifying Grace.—*Publisher,* 2013.

of the Lord—the Church, the Church, I am in the bosom of the true Church. Since the Church is holy, and the pillar of truth, it is our duty to live holily, as well as to believe truly; for, to commit crimes in the house of God, is to defile His sanctuary, and to render oneself doubly guilty. And who is unaware that the servant who knew the will of his Master, and did not trouble himself to perform it, deserved a double chastisement?

We should fear, said St. Francis de Sales, the judgments of God, but without discouragement, and take courage at the sight of His mercies, but without presumption. Those who have an excessive and inordinate fear of being damned show plainly that they have great need of humility and submission. We must indeed abase, annihilate, lose ourselves, but this ought to be to gain, preserve, save ourselves. That humility which is prejudicial to charity, is assuredly a false humility. Such is that which leads to trouble, to discouragement, to despair; for it is contrary to charity, which, while commanding us *to work out our salvation with fear and trembling,* forbids us at the same time to diffide in the goodness of God, who desires the conversion and salvation of all.

3. THE SOULS IN PURGATORY

The opinion of St. Francis de Sales, says the Bishop of Belley, was that, from the thought of Purgatory, we should draw more consolation than pain. The greater number of those, he said, who fear Purgatory so much, do so in consideration of their own interests, and of the love they bear themselves rather than the interests of God, and this happens because those who treat of this place from the pulpit usually speak of its pains, and are silent of the happiness and peace which are found in it.

No doubt the torments are so great that the greatest sufferings of this life cannot be compared with them; but still, the interior satisfaction there is such, that no enjoyment or prosperity on earth can equal it.

The souls in Purgatory are in a constant state of union with God.

They are perfectly submissive to His will, or, to speak better, their will is so transformed into the will of God, that they cannot wish for anything but what God wishes; in such a manner, that if Paradise were opened to them, they would rather precipitate themselves into Hell than appear before God with the stains which they still perceive on themselves.

They are purified voluntarily and lovingly, because such is the divine good pleasure. The souls in Purgatory are there indeed for their sins, sins which they have detested, and sovereignly detested; but as to the abjection and pain that still remain, of being detained there, and deprived for a time of the joy of the blessed in Paradise, they endure all that lovingly, and devoutly pronounce this canticle of the divine justice: "Thou art just, O Lord, and thy judgment is right."

They wish to be there in the manner that pleases God, and for as long a time as He pleases.

They are impeccable, and cannot have the least motion of impatience, or be guilty of the smallest imperfection.

They love God more than themselves, and more than

all things else, with a perfect, pure, and disinterested love.

They are consoled by angels.

They are assured of their salvation.

Their most bitter bitterness is in the most profound peace.

If Purgatory is a kind of Hell as regards pain, it is a kind of Paradise as regards the sweetness which charity diffuses through the heart—charity which is stronger than death, and more powerful than Hell, and whose lamps are fire and flames.

A state more desirable than terrible, since its flames are flames of love.

Terrible, nevertheless, since they postpone the end of all consummation, which consists in seeing and loving God, and in this vision and love, to praise and glorify Him for all eternity. With regard to this subject, St. Francis de Sales approved very much of the admirable *Treatise on Purgatory,* written by the blessed Catherine of Genoa.

If these things be so, I shall be asked, why recommend so much the souls in Purgatory to our charity?

The reason is, because, notwithstanding their advantages, the state of these souls is still very sad and truly deserving of compassion, and, moreover, the glory which they will render to God in Heaven is delayed. These two motives ought to engage us, by our prayers, our fasts, our alms, and all kinds of good works, especially by offering the Holy Sacrifice of the Mass for them, to procure their speedy deliverance.

When any of St. Francis de Sales' friends or acquaintances died, he never grew weary of speaking fondly of them, or recommending them to the prayers of others.

His usual expression was: "We do not remember sufficiently our dead, our faithful departed;" and the proof of it is, that we do not speak enough of them. We turn away from that discourse as from a sad subject, we leave the dead to bury their dead; their memory perishes from us with the sound of their mourning bell; we forget that the friendship which ends, even with death, is never true, Holy Scripture assuring us that true love is stronger than death.

He was accustomed to say that in this single work of mercy, the thirteen others are assembled.

Is it not, he said, in some manner, to visit the sick, to obtain by our prayers the relief of the poor suffering souls in Purgatory?

Is it not to give drink to those who thirst after the vision of God, and who are enveloped in burning flames, to share with them the dew of our prayers?

Is it not to feed the hungry, to aid in their deliverance by the means which faith suggests?

Is it not truly to ransom prisoners?

Is it not to clothe the naked, to procure for them a garment of light, a raiment of glory?

Is it not an admirable degree of hospitality, to procure their admission into the heavenly Jerusalem, and to make them fellow citizens with the saints and domestics of God?

Is it not a greater service to place souls in Heaven, than to bury bodies in the earth?

As to spirituals, is it not a work whose merit may be compared to that of counseling the weak, correcting the wayward, instructing the ignorant, forgiving offences, enduring injuries? And what consolation, however great, that can be given to the afflicted of this world, is comparable with that which is brought by our prayers, to those poor souls who have such bitter need of them?

4. MOTIVES ON ACCOUNT OF WHICH IMPERFECT CHRISTIANS OUGHT NOT TO FEAR THEIR PASSAGE TO ETERNITY, AND MAY EVEN DESIRE IT [4]

As the Christian life is only an imitation and expression of the life which Jesus Christ led for us, so the Christian death ought to be only an imitation and expression of the death which Jesus Christ endured for us. Jesus Christ died to satisfy the justice of God for the sins of all men, and to put an end to the reign of iniquity, to render to His Father the most perfect obedience, by submitting to the sentence of death justly pronounced against all sinners, whose place He held, to render by His death an infinite homage to the majesty of God, and to acknowledge His sovereign dominion over all creatures. Every Christian is obliged to accept death in these same dispositions, and should esteem himself only too happy in the thought that Jesus Christ wished to unite the Sacrifice of His divine life, infinitely more precious than the lives of all men and angels, with the sacrifice which each one of us should make to God of our miserable and unworthy life, and that He wished to render our death,

---

4   We have so often met, in the exercise of our holy ministry, with souls who have an excessive fear of death, that we have thought it a duty to add to the consoling reflections of St. Francis de Sales another chapter, the most solid we know on the subject. [This note and this section appear to have been written by Fr. Huguet, the compiler.—*Publisher,* 2013.]

by uniting it with His, capable of meriting for us an eternal life. To die without participating in these dispositions of Jesus Christ at death, is not to die as a Christian, it is to die of necessity as a beast, it is to die as the reprobate.[5]

Every Christian is obliged to labor for the acquisition of these dispositions during his whole life, which is only given him to learn how to die well. We should often adore in Jesus Christ that ardent zeal which He had to satisfy the justice of God and to destroy sin, that spirit of obedience and sacrifice in which He lived and died, and which He still retains in the mystery of the Eucharist. We should ask Him to share it with us, especially during the time of the Holy Sacrifice of the Mass and Communion, when Jesus Christ offers Himself again to His Father in these same dispositions, and comes to us to communicate them to us. The more we participate in these holy dispositions, the less we shall fear a death which ought to be most precious and meritorious before God, and which will be the more so, as we shall more fully enter into the designs of Jesus Christ, who, dying really but once, to render to His Father the supreme honor which was due to Him, desired to offer to Him till the end of ages the death of each of His members, as a continuation of His sacrifice.

One of the chief effects of the Incarnation and death of Jesus Christ has been to deliver us from the fear of death: He became man, and a mortal man, *that He might destroy by His death him who was the prince of death, that is to say, the devil, and that He might deliver those whom the fear of*

---

5   A Christian would implicitly participate in these dispositions simply by being in the state of grace.—*Publisher*, 2013.

death held in continual servitude during life. Is it not in some manner to dishonor the victory of Jesus Christ over death, to tremble before an enemy whom He has vanquished, and to remain still in slavery through fear of dying?

Jesus Christ ardently desired the arrival of the hour that would consummate His sacrifice, by the effusion of His blood: "I have a baptism," so He calls His Passion, "wherewith I am to be baptized, and how am I straitened until it be accomplished!" Should not a Christian, who has the honor of being one of His members, enter into His spirit, and desire the accomplishment of the baptism with which he is to be baptized? For death ought to appear to the true Christian as a baptism, in which he is to be washed from all his sins, and regenerated to a life of immortality, perfectly exempt from every corruption of sin. We should, then, like Jesus, desire with ardor to sacrifice our life as soon as possible: firstly, to render to the sovereign majesty of God, and all His divine perfections, the greatest glory that any creature can render to Him, and to render the most perfect homage to the death of Jesus Christ, our God and Saviour; secondly, to offer to God the most worthy thanksgiving, in gratitude for having sacrificed for us the life of His Son on the cross, as well as for having continued during so many ages to immolate His Body and Blood on our altars, and in gratitude for having given us His Holy Spirit and the life of grace, which is more precious than all the lives in the world; thirdly, to offer to God the fullest satisfaction that we are able to offer Him for our sins, by offering Him our death in union with that of Jesus Christ; fourthly, to draw down upon ourselves the greatest mercies of God, by an humble acceptance of death, and by the continual sacrifice which we shall make to Him of our life. For, although our life is so vile a thing, so little worthy of being offered to God in sacrifice, defiled as it is with so many sins, yet it is the most considerable present we can make to Him; and God is so good as to receive this remnant of sin, as a sacrifice of sweet odor.

A countless number of martyrs, of every age, sex, and country, have run to death with joy, and looked upon it as their greatest happiness to be able to sacrifice themselves for God in the midst of the most dreadful torments. The pagan or irregular life which some among them had led previously did not stay their ardor; because they hoped by their death entirely to repair the past. "Why," says St. Jerome, "do we not imitate them in something?" Are we not, like them, the disciples of a God crucified for our salvation, and destined to the same kingdom of Heaven? It is true that we have not, like them, the happiness of offering to God a bloody death; but, why should we not endeavor to supply its place, by the continual oblation that we can make to Him of the kind of death which He destines for us? "For I venture to say," adds this holy father, "that there is as much, and perhaps more, merit in offering to Him our life during the successive moments in which He preserves it to us, than in losing it once by the cruelty of executioners. The sacrifice which we make to God of our life, if sincere, is the greatest act of love that we can make." St. Augustine says: "If the angels could envy any privilege in man, it is his ability to die for the love of God."

We ask of God every day that His kingdom should

come. This kingdom of God will be perfectly established in us only by death, which will be for each of us an end to sin, the destruction of concupiscence, and the beginning of the absolute reign of justice and charity. To ask of God, every day, the coming of His kingdom, and, at the same time, to fear death excessively—are these things easily allied? The desire of the kingdom of God and of eternal life is essential to salvation. "It is not sufficient," says St. Augustine, "to believe by faith in a blessed life, we must love it by charity, and wish that we were already in the celestial abode; and it is impossible to have these dispositions in the heart, without being glad to depart from this life." At the commencement of the divine prayer in which we ask of God the coming of His kingdom, He orders us to say to Him: "Our Father, Who art in Heaven." If we sincerely believe that God is our Father, and we His children, how can we fear to go to our Heavenly Father, in order to reign with Him, to enjoy His possessions, and to repose forever on His bosom?

The Scripture represents all the faithful as so many persons who expect the last coming of Jesus Christ, who love His coming, and who go forward to meet Him as far as lies in them by their groans and desires. Why are we Christians? Why are we converted to God? "It is," says St. Paul, "to serve the true and living God, and to expect the Heaven of His Son Jesus, whom He has raised up, and who has delivered us from the wrath to come." To whom will the Lord, *as a just judge, render the crown of justice on the great day?* The same Apostle answers, that it will be *to those who love His coming. Since the earth, and all that it contains, must be consumed by fire,* which will precede the coming of the great Judge, "What ought you to be, says St. Peter to all the faithful, "And what ought to be the sanctity of your life, the piety of your actions, awaiting, and, as it were, hastening by your desires, the coming of the day of the Lord?" Jesus Christ, after having given a description of the frightful signs which will precede His coming, after having told us that men will wither away for fear in expectation of the evils with which the world of the impious will be threatened, addresses immediately to all His disciples who were present, and to all those who should follow Him during the course of ages, these sweet words of consolation and joy: "As for you, when these things begin to happen, look up, and lift up your heads, because your redemption is at hand. . . . When you shall see these things come to pass, know that the kingdom of God is nigh." The great maxims which the Apostles and Jesus Christ Himself teach us, accord perfectly with an ardent desire of death; but do they accord with an excessive fear of death? Are we not afraid to dishonor those great truths, by the opposition that we show between the dispositions which they require, and those which we entertain? "Jesus Christ," says St. Augustine, "will share His kingdom with all those who shall have sincerely desired that His kingdom should come." "He will render," says the Apostle, "the crown of justice to those who love His coming." What, then, should we desire more than His arrival, since it is the sure means of our reigning with Him?

Many persons are tormented at death with the remembrance of their crimes, and, seeing that they have done no penance, they are tempted to despair. "Oh, if I had fasted! Oh, if I had performed great charities for the poor! Alas! I am no longer in a state to perform them. What will become of me? What shall I do?" You can do something greater than all you have mentioned, namely, accept death, and unite it with that of Jesus Christ. There is no mortification comparable to this: it is the deepest humiliation, the greatest impoverishment, the most terrible penance; and I do not at all doubt but that he who is grieved for having offended God, and who accepts death willingly in satisfaction for his sins, will immediately obtain pardon. What a consolation to be able to perform while dying a greater penance than all the anchorets have been able to perform in deserts, and this at a time when one would seem no longer able to do anything! What a pity to see an innumerable multitude of persons deprive themselves of the fruit of death, which of all the pains of life is the one of most merit! *Ut quid perditio haec?*[6] Why waste so advantageous an occasion of honoring God, satisfying His justice, discharging one's debts, and purchasing Heaven?

I acknowledge that your life is nothing in comparison with that of Our Lord Jesus Christ; but, when offered through love, it is of inestimable value. What does God care about an alms of two farthings? Yet the poor widow, in the Gospel, who gave it, deserved to be praised by the Son of God, and to be preferred to the Scribes and Pharisees, who had given much more considerable alms, because, says He, she has given all that she had, and, notwithstanding her poverty, has given it with a great heart. *Haec de penuria*

---

6   "To what purpose is this waste?" (*Matt.* 26:8).—*Publisher, 2013.*

sua omnia quae habuit misit totum victum suum.[7]

We can say the same of him who gives his life to God: he gives all that he has, without reserving anything, and this is what renders death precious. This is what made the early Christians run with so much eagerness to martyrdom: they all wished to give back to Our Lord the life which they had received from Him, and to compensate by their death for that which He had endured for love of them.

We can no longer be martyrs; oh, what an affliction! but still we can die for Jesus Christ! We have a life that we can lose for His love! Oh, what a consolation!

The line of distinction which St. Augustine draws between the perfect and the imperfect is that the perfect suffer life with pain and receive death with joy, while the imperfect receive death only with patience, struggling against themselves to submit to the will of God: preferring however to yield to what He requires of them, arming themselves with courage to overcome the desire of life, and to receive death with submission and peace.

Perfection, therefore, consists in desiring to die, that we may no longer be imperfect, that we may wholly cease to offend God, that God may reign perfectly in us, and that this body of sin, which we carry about with us until death, may, in punishment of its continual revolts against God, be reduced to dust, fully to satisfy His justice and sanctity, and, by this last and most profound humiliation, fully to repair all the injuries which it has committed against the Divine Majesty. We rise towards perfection in proportion as these

---

7   "She of her want cast in all she had, even her whole living." (Cf. *Mark* 12:44). —*Publisher,* 2013.

holy desires of death become more ardent and sincere, and the quickest means of becoming perfect is to desire death with one's whole heart.

The preparations that we might wish to bring with us to our last sacrifice ought not, when the hour of consummating it arrives, to lead us to desire that the sacrifice should be deferred. These preparations are less necessary than submission to the will of God. Our submission can supply the place of these preparations, but nothing can supply the want of our submission; a thing which souls, even the most imperfect, should never forget. It is more advantageous for us to appear before Jesus Christ, when He announces His coming, than to expose ourselves to the risk of meeting Him too late, by expecting that we shall afterwards be better prepared. The essential preparation is to go before Him with confidence and love; and we must think only of exciting acts of these virtues. It ought to be a great subject of humiliation and confusion to us, not to feel a holy ardor and impatience to go to Him. Happy are we, says St. Chrysostom, if we sigh and groan continually within ourselves, awaiting the accomplishment of our divine adoption, which will be the redemption and deliverance of our bodies and souls—if we desire to depart from this world with as much ardor and impatience as the banished desire an end of their exile, and captives of their imprisonment.[8] This impatience, adds the holy doctor, which we testify to God, will serve much to obtain the pardon of our sins, and will be the best of all dispositions for appearing before Him.

---

8 Chrys., *Hom. xvii in Gen. et alib.*

We have elsewhere shown that no person, however holy his life may have been, should rely upon his virtues, if God should examine them without mercy. It is to be already condemned, to consent to be judged without a great mercy. Confidence in the divine mercy, and in the merits of Jesus Christ, is the only security for all. Since, then, we must always return to this point, let us, from this moment, abandon ourselves to these dispositions in life and in death. Let us hold, as a certain truth, that the more fully we thus abandon ourselves, the more just shall we be, and the more agreeable our sacrifices to God.